THE MAN WHO
DECIPHERED
LINEAR B

Andrew Robinson

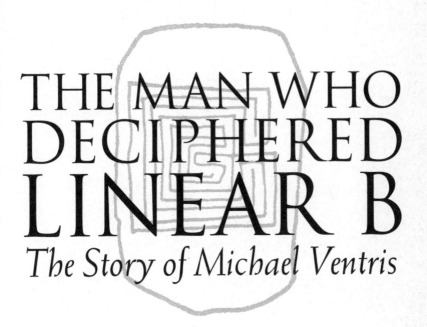

THE MAN WHO DECIPHERED LINEAR B

The Story of Michael Ventris

With over 40 illustrations

Thames & Hudson

To the memory of Antony Coulthard (1918–45),
a gifted linguist and the uncle I never knew

First published in hardcover in the United States of America in 2002 by
Thames & Hudson Inc., 500 Fifth Avenue, New York, New York 10110

thamesandhudsonusa.com

First paperback edition 2012

Library of Congress Catalog Card Number 2001096319
ISBN 978-0-500-28998-3

Printed and bound in China by Toppan Leefung

Contents

Acknowledgments

I first became interested in Michael Ventris in 1989, while researching a television programme about his decipherment of Linear B. Although the programme was not made, I found myself writing a few pages about the decipherment in my 1995 book, *The Story of Writing*, and becoming curious about the somewhat shadowy personality behind the achievement. I also became friendly with his collaborator John Chadwick, author of *The Decipherment of Linear B*, who helped me considerably until his death in 1998.

While writing this small book, which is obviously not a full biography, it has been pleasant to discover that Ventris's generosity and cooperative spirit live on nearly half a century after his death. I have enjoyed invaluable help from his surviving friends and from younger admirers of all that he achieved in his short life, in both decipherment and architecture.

In the world of classical studies, I am indebted to Alicia Totolos, former secretary of the Institute of Classical Studies in London, who went to great trouble to make available Ventris's letters and papers, including the press coverage of the decipherment; to John Killen, emeritus professor of Mycenaean Greek at Cambridge University, a close associate of John Chadwick, who put Chadwick's papers on the decipherment at my disposal; and to Tom Palaima, professor of classics at the University of Texas at Austin, who sent me copies of Ventris's letters to Emmett Bennett Jr and Alice Kober from his PASP archives. All three also shared with me their personal knowledge of the subject.

In the world of architecture, Oliver Cox, a close friend of Ventris as a student at the Architectural Association school, was constantly encouraging and put me in touch with architects and others who knew Ventris. These include Colin Boyne, Dargan Bullivant, Michael Grice, David Medd and Edward Samuel, to all of whom I am grateful, especially Colin Boyne, former editor of the *Architects' Journal*, and Dargan Bullivant, both of whom provided essential background for understanding Ventris's final architectural project.

Among the Ventris family, I am grateful to his grandson Björn Ventris (son of the late Nikki Ventris) and Björn's mother Renee Ventris, who showed me papers and photographs and discussed Ventris's family life; to his daughter Tessa Ventris, who kindly granted permission to quote from Ventris's letters and writings; and to Carol Horton, half-sister of Lois Ventris.

Grateful thanks are also due to Dr John Bennet (of Oxford University) and Tony Meredith (of Stowe School) for essential help, and to Prof. Emmett Bennett Jr, Prof. Sir John Boardman, Jean Cox, Prof. Eric Handley, Rachel and Sinclair Hood, the late Patrick Hunter, Prof. Maurice Pope, Dr Tessa Rajak, John Renton, Robin Richards, Dr Sue Sherratt, Dr John Simopoulos and the late Prudence Smith.

Finally, I thank the staff of Thames & Hudson for the care and intelligence they have shown in producing the book. Jamie Camplin, my longstanding editor, deserves a personal mention, even though he has a Ventris-like reticence about being acknowledged. He is certainly among the best there is.

London, August 2001

Introduction

'There is a land called Crete, set in the wine-dark sea, lovely and
fertile and ocean-rounded. Those who live in this land are many,
indeed past counting, and there are ninety cities there. The population
speaks many tongues; there are Achaeans, there are the brave True
Cretans, the Cydonians, the triply divided Dorians and the noble
Pelasgians. Among the cities is mighty Knossos; its king was once
Minos, who every ninth year took counsel with Zeus himself.'

Odysseus in Homer's *Odyssey*, Book XIX

A mere two hundred years ago, the world's oldest known languages were Greek, Latin and Hebrew. History, in the sense
of readable written records, began no earlier than about
600 B.C. Although the antiquity of inscriptions in Egypt and the Near
East was suspected, nothing definite could be said about it, beyond what
was written in those parts of the Old Testament that seemed historical,
and in the confusing accounts of ancient historians and geographers such
as Herodotus and Strabo. The age of civilization in India, China and the
Americas was *terra incognita*.

But then, around 1805, a French schoolboy, Jean-François Champollion, seeing some of the treasures just brought back from Egypt by
Napoleon's savants, became determined to decipher the Egyptian hieroglyphs. Twenty years later, with the help of the Rosetta stone, Champollion succeeded and was able to read the script of the pharaohs; as a direct
result, the historical time span was doubled, extending back to about

3000 B.C. Later in the 19th century, the cuneiform scripts of Mesopotamia were also deciphered; and scholars were able to understand a range of Near Eastern tongues and read the records and literature of ancient Sumer, Babylon and Assyria, comparable in age with those of Egypt.

Europe, however, still seemed to possess no civilization older than the glories of classical Greece – unless one included the tantalizing stories of the Trojan war composed by Homer at an uncertain date and orally transmitted to later writers. Heinrich Schliemann's famous excavations at Troy and Mycenae in the 1870s, stimulated by his passion for Homer, put paid to that mistaken impression for ever. Here were golden treasures and a powerful citadel with a Lion Gate worthy of Homer's King Agamemnon, belonging to a Bronze Age civilization dating to 1400–1200 B.C or earlier: clear evidence, thought some archaeologists (including Schliemann himself, to begin with), that the Mycenaeans were Greeks, ancestors of the founders of western civilization. But the experts in classical Greek art were unconvinced by the new finds which they thought generally barbaric, and the classical philologists were offered no Mycenaean inscriptions to decipher and learn the Mycenaean language from. For no writing had been found at Mycenae by a disappointed Schliemann: not even fragments, certainly no hoped-for record of the Trojan war. It appeared that the Mycenaeans were illiterate, and not Greek speakers, and that there was no continuity between the newly discovered civilization and the classical Greeks who wrote with an alphabet, the ancestor of our modern alphabets.

Then, a century ago, in 1900, Arthur Evans began to dig up and reconstruct the 'great city' of Knossos mentioned by Homer, at a site in the northern part of central Crete. He discovered what he believed was the palace of King Minos, with its notorious labyrinth, legendary home of the Minotaur. Over the next three decades, Evans spent his family fortune on reconstructing the palace, including its 'Room of the Throne' and its brilliantly painted frescoes, and fell in love with 'his' Minoans.

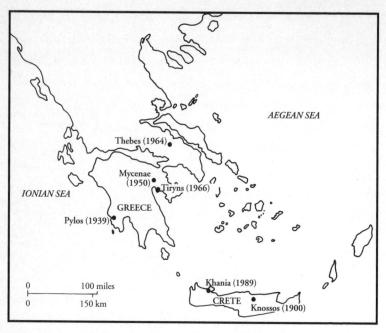

The locations and dates of Linear B tablet discoveries.

Just as they had enthralled Homer and the ancient Greeks, the Minoans in their beautiful island dazzled Evans, too, and convinced him that Greece was 'a Mainland branch of the Minoan culture', a mere 'Minoan plantation'. So much for the greatness of classical Greece and the grandeur and gold of Mycenae and Troy excavated by Schliemann – said Evans in effect: it was the Minoans, and not the Mycenaeans or the Greeks, who had created the first great European civilization; and it was he who had revealed it to a wondering world. If any classical specialist – such as the archaeologists digging in mainland Greece at places such as Mycenae – disagreed with Evans, they seldom voiced their opinion, such was Sir Arthur's prestige and influence as one of the two or three best-known archaeologists of his time. When the director of the British School at Athens, A. J. B. (Alan) Wace, ventured to differ from Evans in 1923, he had to retire from his position and was excluded from digging in Greece for a considerable period. Minoan hegemony over Greece (and Evans's hegemony over practically every scholar in the field) became the orthodoxy.

And Evans, unlike Schliemann, found writing – the earliest writing in Europe. 'Linear Script of Class B', which is nowadays dated to *c.* 1450 B.C., two or three centuries before the Trojan war, was the name given by Evans to the fairly primitive characters scratched on clay tablets that he discovered soon after he began (and which other archaeologists much later on were surprised to discover at places on the mainland, including Mycenae). The 'Class B' label was to distinguish the characters from similar-looking but nevertheless distinct characters on archaeologically older tablets (now dated to 1750–1450 B.C.) that Evans had labelled 'Linear Script of Class A', which had been found at Knossos but chiefly at another Minoan palace excavation in southern Crete. 'Linear' – not because the symbols were written in sequence but because they consisted of lines inscribed on a surface, as opposed to the three-dimensional, engraved images of a third, pictographic Cretan script, found chiefly on seal stones and only in the eastern part of the island, which Evans dubbed 'Hieroglyphic' but which actually did not much resemble Egyptian writing.

Portrait of Arthur Evans, and a Linear B tablet he published in 1900.

To be frank, Linear B tablets are uninspiring objects to the eye of the uninitiated, unlike Egyptian hieroglyphic inscriptions, the Mayan glyphs of Central America and many of the cuneiform tablets. They are flat, smooth pieces of clay, their colour generally dull grey but sometimes like red brick (the result of greater oxidation when the tablet was burnt). Their sizes vary from small sealings and labels little more than an inch across to heavy, page-shaped tablets designed to be held in a single hand, the largest being as big as a fair-sized paperback. Evans found many of them in a fragile, even friable condition and once accidentally reduced a batch to an indecipherable muddy mess by leaving them overnight in a storeroom with a leaky roof.

Indeed, the first traces of Linear B he unearthed were so unimpressive that he copied them and filed them away in what he termed 'a suspense account'. Yet Evans, whose first love was for epigraphy not archaeology – scripts not potsherds, so to speak – quickly became hooked on the problem of what the undeciphered characters meant. They bore little resemblance to Egyptian hieroglyphs (though Evans detected some), and no resemblance to cuneiform or the later Greek alphabet. As for the underlying language of the mysterious Linear inscriptions, Evans was quite convinced, for reasons already given, that it could not be Greek: he therefore coined the term Minoan for it. Then he spent the last 40 years of his long life hoping to decipher the script and language – while keeping the vast majority of the tablets away from other scholars, lest (as one is almost compelled to assume) they got to the answer before the grand old man of Minoan culture.

Michael Ventris, the person who eventually 'cracked' Linear B and discovered it was actually an archaic dialect of Greek – in 1952–53, a decade after Evans's death – was not a professional scholar (unlike, say, Champollion); he was an architect by training who never attended a university and treated Linear B as a kind of hobby that gripped him as a schoolboy. A second irony is that Ventris succeeded where professional scholars failed by being as candid in his decipherment methods as they (and this would include Champollion) were habitually secretive: indeed he kept his 'rivals' literally posted on what he was doing by mailing them detailed 'Work Notes' showing his latest thinking and inviting their criticism and suggestions. Yet a third irony is that Ventris was largely *un*interested in classical literature; it was the problem, the puzzle, of deciphering Linear B that fascinated him, not so much what the inscriptions might tell us about ancient Greece (again unlike Champollion, who was passionate about all things ancient Egyptian).

If there is one word that sums up Ventris, it is 'unconventional'. Almost everyone who knew him remarked on the ease and charm of his company, but he could be exceptionally withdrawn and uncommunicative; he was a dazzling polyglot who took pride in speaking most major European languages, yet he felt close to hardly anyone, and these few were mainly English speakers; as an architect and decipherer he believed firmly in collaboration and cross-fertilization, yet he kept his many personal relationships in remarkably separate compartments; his tastes in architecture were thoroughly modern and anti-classical, but his interest in Linear B required an intimate knowledge of the classical world; he had a substantial private income, but he was not interested in living the lifestyle of the rich and had socialist tendencies; even physically he looked much more like a tanned, glamorous sportsman (he was an avid skier) than an etiolated scholar, a City gent far more than an absent-minded professor. It would be easy to continue with this list of paradoxes. Above all, Ventris showed a modesty which verged on diffidence – 'almost alarmingly' so, according to an architect friend – despite having as much (indeed more) to boast about as a Nobel prize winner.

Without a shadow of doubt, this freedom from orthodox thinking and attitudes was the key to Ventris's success as a decipherer of Linear B (though not, it would seem, success in his career as an architect, where he had a long struggle with his excessively logical mind). But it is difficult to pinpoint exactly how the key unlocked the ancient symbols. John Chadwick, the distinguished Cambridge University classicist who was Ventris's academic collaborator in applying the decipherment to the Linear B tablets in the months and years after Ventris had achieved his pioneering breakthrough, made a stab at explaining the working of the magic in 1983, a quarter of a century after Ventris's tragic death at the age of only 34. Chadwick wrote: 'The achievement of the decipherment...required painstaking analysis and sound judgment, but at the same time an element of genius, the ability to take a leap in the dark, but then to find firm ground on the other side. Few discoveries are made solely by processes of logical deduction. At some point the researcher is obliged to chance a guess, to venture an unlikely hypothesis; what matters is whether he can control the leap of the imagination, and have the honesty to evaluate the results soberly. Only after the leap has been made is it possible to go back over the working and discover the logical basis which provided the necessary springboard.'

This is honest, if daunting; it is no accident that Chadwick once confessed to Ventris that he was the 'pedestrian' Dr Watson to the master decipherer's Holmes. Nevertheless, in writing his justly celebrated book *The Decipherment of Linear B* (1958) soon after Ventris had died, Chadwick attempted to turn the decipherment into a more rational process than he knew it actually to have been. Admirably clear though Chadwick's account is, it deliberately underrates the irrational intuitions that pepper Ventris's own Work Notes and hardly mentions most of the blind alleys that Ventris followed – notably his sustained conviction, to the very end of the chase, that the 'Minoan' language of Linear B could *not* be Greek but must be related to Etruscan, a barely understood, non-Indo-European language.

One can well understand why Chadwick did this, given the need to make complex material clear to the general reader, and, as important, the natural academic desire to prefer reasoned explanation over mystification and words like 'genius'. Less understandable, perhaps, is his book's omission of the human factor: the way in which Ventris's unconventional personality strongly influenced his approach to Linear B. But then, as Chadwick himself admitted, he knew 'only one side of [Ventris's] character', and their relationship was 'largely through letters'. Of Ventris's extraordinary linguistic gifts in modern European languages, Chadwick at least had some slight first-hand experience, but of his novel, sophisticated, analytical approach to design in architecture – which Ventris applied to the decipherment too – Chadwick knew next to nothing; he therefore left the architect totally out of his book. It was really not possible for Chadwick – and no doubt he felt the academic's typical aversion towards mixing the man with the work – to grasp fully the diverse and unique influences that drove Ventris. While he had personal experience of the fact that Ventris's 'brain worked with astonishing rapidity, so that he could think out all the implications of a suggestion almost before it was out of your mouth', it was altogether another thing to explain this brilliance – if it can be explained.

I am not so immodest as to think I can explain it. But I am certain that we do understand the decipherment better by interweaving Ventris's life with the details of Linear B, as I have done in this book. Besides, we all have a natural curiosity to know how genius differs from ourselves. And I have no doubt that Ventris was a genius. His decipherment did not open up the riches of a glittering civilization like Champollion's, or the weird universe of the ancient Maya, as revealed by the decipherment of the Mayan glyphs in the late 20th century. The decipherment of Linear B is, however, generally regarded as the greatest intellectual achievement in archaeological decipherment ever – comparable with the discovery of DNA's structure by Crick and Watson, which curiously occurred at the same time in 1952–53. And in my view the man who achieved it, Michael Ventris, is the most intriguing of all the individuals to have had the honour of 'cracking' the script of an ancient culture.

1
An Unconventional Upbringing

'Did you say the tablets haven't been deciphered, Sir?'
Michael Ventris as a schoolboy to Sir Arthur Evans at an exhibition
on the Minoan world, 1936

To English ears, Ventris is a name that sounds slightly foreign, its origin hard to determine – perhaps appropriately for a man like Michael Ventris. Yet the Ventrises are a long-established English family. *The Dictionary of National Biography* lists, apart from Michael, Sir Peyton Ventris, a judge who was member of parliament for Ipswich in 1689; and that branch of the family, living near Cambridge, can be traced back to 1490. A second branch lived from 1560 to 1700 near Bedford at Compton Manor, a house that still stands; the panelling of its dining room contains bullet holes said to date from the civil war when Henry, brother of Sir Charles Ventris, was killed.

Continuing the tradition, Michael Ventris's paternal grandfather, the son of a clergyman, was a distinguished army officer, the colonel of the Essex Regiment, who served in Africa, India and the Far East, retiring in 1920 as a major-general commanding the British forces in China. And Ventris's father was an officer in the Indian Army. He, however, had an undistinguished career, overshadowed by illness and perhaps his own father's military reputation: he retired from the army in his late thirties, as a lieutenant colonel, and was a semi-invalid for most of his remaining years until his death in 1938.

But Colonel Ventris did break with tradition in one important respect – he married a half-Polish woman, Anna Dorothea Janasz, the daughter of Joseph Janasz, a wealthy landowner in Poland, and an English mother from a Northamptonshire family. A fine-featured, intelligent, sensitive woman – known as 'The Charmer' in her family – who enjoyed fashionable clothes and developed a passion for modern art and design, Dorothea seems to have been a somewhat unsuitable partner for an unremarkable army officer. At any rate, it is she who would bring up their only child and influence him towards languages, archaeology and architecture, and not her husband, who apparently had little significant effect on the boy.

Although Michael was born in England (on 12 July 1922), he would spend much of his childhood on the Continent, chiefly in Switzerland, where his father was seeking treatment

Above, Dorothea Ventris. Below, the Ventris family and friends on holiday in Switzerland, c. 1930.

for tuberculosis. By the time he was just eight years old, he had been at boarding schools for three years: a year in England and about two years in Switzerland. Since the only languages spoken in the Swiss school were French and German, no English, he was compelled to speak both languages (including of course Swiss German). From his mother he picked up Polish. Very soon, it was obvious that Michael had an unusual flair for languages. In adult life, he would learn European languages in a matter of weeks and months; the more languages he spoke, he once told a friend, the easier it became to pick up a new one.

Photographs of him in the Ventris family album around this time show a pretty but slightly forlorn boy, happy with his smiling, chicly dressed mother but solemn with his more distant, melancholy-looking father against a snowy background of Swiss chalets and ski-clad adults. But Michael fell in love with the Swiss landscapes of his early years. Later in life, in wartime, while anxiously awaiting the birth of his first child Nikki, he wrote to his wife: 'The beginning of December was always an exciting part of the year for me as a child – marking the beginning of the white half of the year.... St Nicholas with his shavers of nuts and his rather two-edged little presents always marked a three-star red-letter day in my childhood calendar, even though he was so obviously the peasant from up the mountain, and his beard was only held on precariously against his windy rounds.' His adult passion for skiing dated from this time, though he was never as good a skier as he would have wished.

With such experiences, he could hardly be a typical English public-school boy of the 1930s, especially given his obvious academic talents: he was soon shining in ancient Greek and Latin, in addition to modern languages, at the English preparatory school where his parents sent him when he was nine years old (while continuing to take him regularly to Europe for long periods). Perhaps this is why they chose Stowe School for his secondary education. In 1935, Stowe was a relatively new public school, without too many stuffy traditions, and its energetic, showy headmaster, J. F. Roxburgh, was well known for indulging and encouraging boys with special, even eccentric talents (especially artistic ones) and for opposing the tyranny of athleticism then ruling most public schools. The famous 18th-century buildings and grounds of Stowe – the former estates of the dukes of Buckingham and 'the most sublime setting of any school in England' (Noel Annan, an Old Stoic, but here a fair judge) – also appealed to the Ventris parents, though ironically the school's neoclassical grandeur would help to push their precocious son towards modern architecture.

Michael won a scholarship and spent four years at Stowe, from 1935 to 1939. He did well academically but not outstandingly considering his later achievements. Like many truly original minds, he was not fond of formal schooling, though he never rebelled openly against it. His tutor for his last two years at Stowe when he specialized in classics, P. G. Hunter (inevitably known as 'Piggy'), described him in an obituary as 'neither rebel nor recluse' and in his retirement recalled a boy who had a 'perceptive and clear intelligence, and (when interested) a capacity for taking infinite trouble.' For instance he produced an orographical map of Greece, modelled in clay on a wooden base, 'exquisitely coloured and very neatly lettered' with a dedicatory Greek inscription of 'typical humour', and – this was the hardest part – with 'very convincing' relief. These were all qualities that he would later display in architecture and decipherment, not to speak of map-making as an RAF navigator during the second world war.

Ventris would keep in touch with his former tutor Hunter, whom he liked, when he was working on Linear B in the 1940s and 1950s – uniquely among those who had taught him at Stowe. The rest of the school's staff, including Roxburgh, seem to have held little interest for him. In a letter to a much older Russian friend living in England (the sculptor Naum Gabo) written in March 1939, during his last year at school, Michael gave a glimpse of his true feelings, remarkably mature for his age. He described an 'irritatingly imperialistic' history master, who asked him in class 'whether I wouldn't feel personally humiliated if Britain suffered some insult or had her colonies removed, and when I found some difficulty in agreeing with him, he rebuked me and said that things hadn't gone so far as to allow people to feel no pride in their country. But then five minutes later he told us with a superior grin on his

face that England was the only country who always emerged from a war
with more than she started with, although she professed to be completely
disinterested, implying that England's sense of honour wasn't all it was
made out to be.' Then Michael summed up the master: 'He's quite nice
really but awfully English.'

A few years later, Ventris told his wife that 'I think they [at Stowe]
rather thought me a black sheep.' But there is no real evidence of this;
indeed in the 1980s, Stowe School produced an affectionate booklet
about Ventris, *Michael Ventris Remembered*, in which his contemporaries
recalled how pleasant and humorous he had been as a boy. But it is true
that he stayed in touch with none of them as an adult, and that almost
everyone who knew him at school found him a bit of a mystery. He was
clearly detached from school life and certainly not a team player (his only
sport seems to have been a little fencing): more of an amused, and sometimes amusing, observer of school rituals than an active participant. One
contemporary commented: 'I believe he was half Greek.... My most vivid
recollection is of a sardonic but not unkindly smile.... I am sure that
Michael was without guile or vice; he just thought us funny. I think that
this dispassionate view of established belief and behaviour must have
made it much easier for him to start demolishing Arthur Evans's theories
and deciphering the Linear B script.' Christopher Robin Milne (son of
A. A. Milne), a mathematics specialist who shared a study with Ventris for
two terms, remarked: 'What exactly he did with himself, where exactly his
interests lay, what were his hobbies or his hobby horses, I cannot recall....
I would certainly not have guessed either architecture or cryptography.'
And another contemporary, who was in the scholar's form with Ventris,
remembered chiefly that when they were both about 15, in 1937, Michael
'was so impatient to get on with his research that he worked under the
bedclothes by the light of a torch after official "lights-out".'

Long before he went to Stowe, Michael had started reading about
ancient scripts and languages; when he was seven, he had bought and

studied a scholarly book on the Egyptian hieroglyphs written in German. 'He reads quite advanced books on language and archaeology during the holidays', his mother told the headmaster in September 1936 (apropos of a long complaint from her about the 'monotonous and quite unscientifically planned' school food, which Mrs Ventris felt undermined Michael's health and concentration during term time). Barely a month after she wrote this letter, Michael had his first encounter with Linear B.

According to almost every book on the subject (including *The Decipherment of Linear B*), what is supposed to have happened is that the 14-year-old Ventris heard a lecture in London by Sir Arthur Evans on 'The Minoan world', and became interested when Evans mentioned that the Minoan tablets could not be read. What actually happened is more revealing – about the importance of chance in our lives and also Ventris's serendipitous mind.

Undoubtedly there was a grand public lecture by Evans, on 16 October 1936, at Burlington House, home of the Royal Academy of Arts, to celebrate the 50th anniversary of the British School at Athens. But Michael did not attend it. Instead, he was one of a school party of Stowe classicists taken by Patrick Hunter (who had not yet started to teach Michael) to see a Greek and Minoan art exhibition also arranged for the anniversary at Burlington House. Evans, who was by then 85 years old, happened to be present when the boys arrived, and he proved willing to lead them around the Minoan Room with an impromptu running commentary. They reached a glass cabinet containing some clay tablets and Evans remarked that no one had been able to read them, although he himself had tried hard. At this point – a surprised Hunter sharply remembered even in old age – the most junior member of the party 'piped up, very politely' with a question to Evans: 'Did you say the tablets haven't been deciphered, Sir?' If Evans had not been present at the exhibition that day, or if the 14-year-old had never set eyes on a real tablet but merely attended the public lecture (in which the tablets received only the

*Ventris aged 14, Stowe School, 1936,
the year he first encountered Linear B.*

most cursory mention, and Linear B, being undeciphered, no mention at all), who knows? – Michael Ventris might never have become fascinated with the Cretan scripts.

As it was, he himself told the BBC in 1956, after the decipherment, with gentle understatement: 'Some of us thought it would be a change from our set lessons to try and decipher the tablets, but of course we didn't get anywhere. Somehow I've remained interested in the problem ever since.'

But although Evans would fail to decipher Linear B, by 1936 he had published at least some (less than a sixth) of the tablets and taken some comparatively straightforward yet significant steps in the right direction, which he published in his book *The Palace of Minos at Knossos*. The fourth and final volume of this monumental series, published the year before the exhibition, may well have been the one which Michael soon began to study by torchlight under the bedclothes at Stowe and during the school holidays.

For a start, as already mentioned in the Introduction, Evans recognized the existence of at least three distinct scripts in Crete in the second millennium B.C.: Linear A, Linear B and Hieroglyphic. Concentrating on Linear B, which was by far the most plentiful, he identified the short upright lines that frequently recurred near the horizontal lines that divide most tablets, as word dividers:

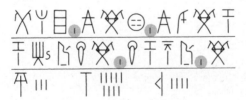

He also worked out the system of counting as follows:

| | = 1 unit | — = 1 ten |
| o = 1 hundred | -φ- = 1 thousand |

Here are two examples of numbers in Linear B tablets, 362 and 1350:

362

1350

Evans also understood that the tablets were inventories, sometimes with a total at the bottom, often involving a pictogram. The fact that the number was a total could be established in the better-preserved tablets by adding up the separate entries above it. Here is an example with the numerals highlighted (ignore the symbols in the top line that appear to be numerals; they are in fact word dividers):

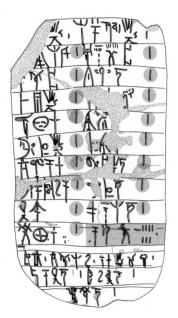

total man 17

And Evans deduced that the two highlighted signs ⊤ ⟩, sometimes ⊤ Υ, common in the Linear B tablets, probably meant 'total'.

Many other pictograms had to be *logograms*, i.e. a sign representing a word; this was clear from their iconic qualities and the fact that they stood out in the tablets because they were accompanied by numerals and were isolated from the majority of other characters:

Man	🯅	Woman	🯆
Horse	🐎	Pig	🐖
Tripod	♒	Cup	🍷
Amphora	🏺	Sword	⚔
Spear	⟍	Arrow	»—→
Chariot	🏎	Wheel	⊛

The tablet opposite, for instance, counts men.

And there were a number of pictograms that came in two forms:

Evans recognized that these stood for male and female animals, presumably counted for the palace of Minos. But he could not determine which pictogram was male and which female.

Such pictograms led Evans astray. In respect of the Linear B signary, he succumbed, at least partially, to one of the commonest errors in decipherment: what might be called 'the pictographic fallacy'. Having gone looking for pictographic elements in the signs, he naturally found them, and then – under the influence of the 'determinatives' found in Egyptian hieroglyphs (such as the 'shepherd's crook' sign in the cartouche of Tutankhamun which 'determines' – i.e. indicates – that it is a ruler's name that is spelt by the cartouche's other signs) – Evans proceeded to treat his supposed Linear B pictograms as logograms referring only to the objects they depicted. Thus ⟙, a frequent sign at the beginning of a word, Evans decided stood for 'double-axe', a common Minoan object with evident religious/ritual significance; and ⟦, which appears five times in the tablet below, stood for 'throne-and-sceptre'. And he went on to conclude that the 'double-axe' sign was a determina-

Minoan double axe, c. 1500 B.C.

tive for words of religious meaning and the 'throne-and-sceptre' sign was a determinative for words of royal meaning.

Given the shape and apparent significance of the double axes and the real throne (of Minos?) that Evans had found at Knossos, both these analogies were not unreasonable, yet his conclusion turned out to be fallacious: the linguistic function of the two signs was actually *phonetic*, not pictographic/logographic as he had postulated (though this fact was not established until well after his death).

There was one other discovery by Evans, of which the young Ventris would have been aware at this time. But we shall postpone it, because it belongs better with Ventris's first published paper on Linear B, written after he had left school.

In the meantime, while learning about Linear B, he was growing up fast in other ways. His mother had divorced his father just after Michael entered Stowe ('I am rather glad to have this opportunity of letting you know about the divorce as Michael would not mention it', Dorothea informed Roxburgh). Not long afterwards, in 1936, mother and son had moved into a flat in north London on Highgate Hill, an area long favoured by architects and close to Hampstead, the intellectual and artistic centre of London in the 1930s, where Dorothea had friends among artists and architects. The move was a huge change. Not only did the flat have a virtually unrivalled view over London, it was brand new and the epitome of *echt* Modernism, being at the top of Highpoint, the block designed by Berthold Lubetkin of Tecton, the Russian émigré architect most famous for his Penguin Pool and other buildings at London Zoo. Supposedly, Highpoint was England's closest approach to a Soviet-style commune: its exterior sheathed in concrete, its interior stripped clean of decorative features, with most services (even the refrigeration) centrally planned, with the emphasis not on Victorian mansion-block privacy but on mid-20th-century communal living – both indoors and in the large, landscaped garden at the back of the building. Modernists raved about Highpoint. A 1937 exhibition at New York's Museum of Modern Art declared it to be 'one of the finest, if not absolutely the finest, middle-class housing projects in the world'. But the ultimate accolade came from Le Corbusier, who told Lubetkin that Highpoint embodied his own theory of the 'vertical garden city'.

The throne room of the palace of Knossos, reconstructed according to Evans's ideas.

Today, with the passing of the modern movement in architecture and the general critical reaction against functionalism and central planning, Highpoint has lost much of its appeal. But even in 1936, some of its admirers were critical. Although Ventris lived there for a long period, until 1953 – and 'cracked' Linear B there – he showed no great enthusiasm for its design, and the house he eventually built for himself off Hampstead Heath does not echo the design of the Highpoint flat in any way. His mother Dorothea went so far as to call Highpoint 'noisy and blatant' in a letter to Marcel Breuer. But she loved the furniture that Breuer had designed for the flat during his brief stay in England in 1935–37 before emigrating to the United States: a chrome and laminate tea trolley, a combined radiogram/sideboard, a bookcase and sideboard with roller fronts, a glass-topped table with tubular metal legs (later used as a work desk for decipherment), a sofa, chairs with broad bentwood arms forming shelves underneath, and other items. 'I count myself extraordinarily fortunate to have this little centre which you made...your interior

Highpoint, Ventris's home from 1936 until 1953, where he deciphered Linear B.

with its shapes and colours and textures of which I never tire. Other people appreciate it too, but no one as much as Michael, who has such a firm affection for his room that I am sure he will never let me give up the flat.' The following year, 1939, she again told him: 'In spite of the fact that we may be going to be bombed to pieces we still have the same enthusiasm for your flat.... We have two new pictures, both by Picasso. One hangs in the dining room, and is flat Cubist, 1923, with very strong masses of brown, grey, white and terracotta against a background of lilac and yellow. The lilac and yellow are marvellous with your blue table.' But she admitted that she had never had the 'courage or inspiration' to introduce into the interior the kind of small personal touches that she knew Breuer wanted, to make the flat feel like it was hers, rather than a showpiece.

Artistically minded and acutely sensitive though she was, Dorothea Ventris was no artist: one looks in vain for her name among the records of the exciting artistic life of 1930s Hampstead, though she knew personally Naum Gabo, Ben Nicholson, Henry Moore and other local artists, and keenly collected their work. Their strong personalities attracted her but, unlike Michael, she found them overwhelming. 'Perhaps you realized in the end how completely I lack self-confidence,' she told Breuer. 'I know I must have seemed unfriendly and ungrateful. The fact is that I am simply terrified of people. I was in a panic that you would bring your friends here [to the flat] – capable, worldly people...who make me feel a fool. So I just faded out and you thought I was indifferent to your interests. Or being the kind, gentle person you are, you were merely chilled and puzzled.'

Nevertheless, she could be very practical, especially where her son was concerned. Her devotion to him is transparent and she strongly encouraged him when he began to show an interest in studying architecture in his last year at Stowe, despite the likely difficulties of getting trained and finding a job as a modernist architect in 1940s Britain, and the undoubted heavy expense. She wrote to Patrick Hunter: 'You will agree with me that Michael is not very sensitive to literature. He loves language, but his aesthetic taste is stronger in music, in the volumes (or spaces) of architecture and sculpture.'

Influenced by Highpoint, Breuer's designs and the constructivist sculpture of Gabo – who refused to distinguish between sculpture and architecture – Michael had started to subject the sublimely inappropriate neoclassical setting of Stowe to some functional analysis of his own. 'Who has ever heard of a functionally built chapel?' he told Gabo. 'I'm not religious myself but I suppose other boys are...'. He toyed with a design for a public school, which he thought would be 'quite interesting just as a technical study' even though a public school was not 'a progressive institution' – a project which was a sort of precursor of his future, post-war design work for the Ministry of Education. Although nothing much came of all this, the mental effort helped to persuade him (and Gabo, who would become something of a father figure for Michael), during the first half of 1939, that he should abandon the study of classical literature and follow his modernist instincts.

Breuer wrote from Harvard University in July, where he was now teaching, and gave solid advice: that Michael should study at the Architectural Association School in London, which was now more sympathetic to modernism than in the mid-1930s. 'A fresh wind seems to blow there and I am sure it is more useful for *professional* studies than Oxford.' But he agreed with Michael that in England an Oxford education had a special social significance. Other possibilities were Harvard and a technical college in Zurich.

In September, Michael was more or less forced to decide. When the Germans invaded Poland, his mother's Polish father lost all his land, property and income, with a disastrous effect on Dorothea's income. She immediately wrote to Stowe withdrawing Michael (he had intended to stay at least one more term) and asking if the fees for the autumn term could be waived – a request that Roxburgh granted. He also, like Breuer, encouraged Michael to apply for admission to the Architectural Association School; this had remained open despite the outbreak of war, while moving from its central London quarters in Bedford Square to temporary premises outside London, at Hadley Common – luckily not far from Highgate. After taking a crash course in drawing at a local art school that autumn – a 'rather gruelling' experience, Michael told Gabo, since he had done no drawing at Stowe and was not naturally talented as an artist as he was as a linguist – he was accepted at the 'AA' and asked to begin his architectural training in January 1940.

Although his mother was pleased, her thoughts were bleak, dominated by the war. She had already lost her brother in the first world war and her husband was dead; now her father was a refugee in London and her only son, 17 years old in 1939, faced the prospect of military call-up. To Roxburgh she wrote in September that she hoped Michael 'would live to do you credit'. But she told Gabo in November: 'I still shiver at any mention of air raids, but in my calmer moments I am convinced that the fear and horror which Picasso made conscious are a universal deterrent and that no nation will dare to start a campaign against open towns because of the reprisals.' Within less than a year, Dorothea herself would be dead, leaving Michael entirely alone.

2

The War Years

*'One can remain sure that no Champollion is working quietly in
a corner and preparing a full and startling revelation, as no one
has access to sufficient reproductions.'*

Michael Ventris, as an RAF serviceman, in a letter to Sir John Myres, October 1942

At Easter 1940, presumably during a break in his architectural training, Ventris sat down in his room at 47 Highpoint and typed a two-page letter to Sir Arthur Evans of extraordinary self-assurance for someone so young. It began: 'I don't know whether you remember my writing to you a few years ago about some theories I had on the elucidation of Minoan. Actually I was only 15 at the time, and I am afraid my theories were nonsense; but you were very kind and answered my letters. I was convinced that the key would prove to be in Sumerian,' – that is, the earliest-known language of Mesopotamia – 'but I am glad to say I have given these ideas up long ago.' The rest of the letter went on to propose a new candidate language for 'Minoan': 'a dialect closely related to Etruscan'.

Six months later, after tearing up two drafts, Ventris had produced a lengthy, scholarly manuscript about his new theory. As the Germans began to bomb London in early September and the battle of the Atlantic got underway in earnest, he mailed this to the *American Journal of Archaeology*, the leading archaeological journal of the United States. Immediately, it was accepted and rushed into print by the editor in the last number for 1940 under the title 'Introducing the Minoan language' with the wholly unknown author given simply as 'M. G. F. Ventris, London'. He was just 18 years old.

During the decipherment and after, a decade later, Ventris would largely disown this paper, as he had disowned his juvenile letters to Evans, but it is in fact of great interest. Not because its conclusions were correct – they were dead wrong – but because of the light it throws on the workings of its author's unusual mind. The paper's curious mixture of cold logic, scholarly caution, wide reading, wild assertions and imaginative leaps suggests why it would be Ventris, and no ordinary classical scholar, who would eventually decipher Linear B.

At the very beginning, Ventris dismissed what he called 'the fantasy' of a number of scholars 'which makes Minoan out as Greek'. He pointed out the flaws in their methods and noted that their various readings, supposedly all in Greek, were largely unrelated to each other. This was fair and reasonable, but then he let slip his main argument: 'The theory that Minoan could be Greek is based of course on a deliberate disregard for historical plausibility.' In other words, Ventris was consciously taking the same line as Evans, mentioned in the Introduction: that the civilization of the Minoans on Crete was known to be historically earlier and artistically different from that of the Greek mainland at Mycenae, and therefore the Minoan language had to be a pre-Greek language.

In following the same line, Ventris was aware that Evans himself had come dangerously close to the Greek hypothesis for 'Minoan', in volume four of *The Palace of Minos*. There, in search of further clues to the decipherment of Linear B (after he had identified the word dividers, numerals and pictograms), Evans had turned east, to Cyprus. Here was another island on which an ancient script had been found, dating to about 800–200 B.C. But unlike Linear B, the classical Cypriot script had been deciphered (in 1871), because it appeared alongside the classical Greek alphabet in a number of 'bilingual' inscriptions:

To digress for a moment, the spoken language represented in these 'bilinguals' is the same in the case of both scripts: Greek – a dialect of Greek in the Cypriot case. The historical reason for this, according to classicists of Evans's day, was that Greek speakers fleeing the Trojan war had brought Greek to Cyprus. Since the sounds of the Greek alphabetic signs were known, the sounds of the Cypriot script could be deciphered and matched with their corresponding signs. But the Cypriot script turned out to be, not alphabetic, but *syllabic*, with 56 signs, one for each syllable; an inconvenient way to represent Greek sounds, if manageable. The Cypriot syllabary is a so-called 'open' syllabary, in which a syllabic sign stands not for a consonant C but for a consonant with an inherent vowel, CV. (In 'closed' syllabaries, a sign stands for CVC.) This means that when an 'open' syllabic sign is used to represent a final consonant in a word, the sign's inherent vowel must be assumed to be silent, i.e. C(V). In classical Cypriot, therefore, the many words that finish with the syllabic sign ⊢, *se*, have a silent *e* and actually end in *s*, which agrees with a very common ending for words in classical Greek, '-s' (e.g. logo**s**, Dionyso**s**). This was as expected in a dialect of Greek.

Evans, however, was not looking to the Cypriot script for its Greek connections – rather the opposite, given his Minoan predilections. His hope was that the *known* sounds of the Cypriot script could help him to decipher the *unknown* sounds of the Linear B script, but without assuming that the language of Linear B was Greek, or even a dialect of Greek.

His idea may seem somewhat perverse, but it was based on a theory of his that the Cypriot *script* was somehow derived from the 'Minoan' Linear B script, while the Cypriot *language* was *not* derived from the 'Minoan' language. (One might recall the modern Turkish script, which Kemal Atatürk deliberately derived from the roman script, even though the Turkish language is not derived from any European language written in the roman script.) According to Evans, 'Minoan'-speaking people, possibly traders to begin with, must have settled in Cyprus, bringing their script with them from Crete. That was why, he said, some of the Cypriot signs looked so similar to the Linear B signs, despite being up to a thousand or so years younger than Linear B.

Here are the eight most similar signs and their syllabic phonetic values in Cypriot:

Linear B	Cypriot	Cypriot sound values
ㄅ	⟨	*po*
⊦	⊢	*ta*
†	+	*lo*
╤	╤	*to*
⊬	⊬	*se*
╪	╪	*pa*
〒	〒	*na*
⋀	⋀	*ti*

Evans decided to test these values on a promising-looking tablet from Knossos:

He noticed on the tablet six horse heads, two of which were incomplete. (The join in the tablet was made by John Chadwick years after Evans's death, so Evans's drawing below does not include the left-hand portion.) Of the four horse heads in the middle and on the right of the tablet, two had manes and two did not. The ones without manes, foals presumably, were preceded by the same pair of Linear B signs:

According to the Cypriot phonetic values, the two signs should read *po-lo*. What might 'polo' mean in the 'Minoan' language? Evans duly noted that it resembled the classical Greek word 'pōlos', young horse or foal, (and its dual form 'pōlo', two foals); in fact 'foal', the English word, comes from the same source as Greek 'pōlos'. If the 'Minoan' language and the Greek language were related after all, 'Minoan' 'polo' could easily be the equivalent of classical Greek 'pōlos'. The tablet would then mean:

horses 2	*polo* foals
polo foals 2	horses 4

Presumably, the word ˥ † ('polo') had been added by the Minoan scribe to make it absolutely clear that the maneless pictogram was a foal and not an adult animal.

But Evans rejected this plausible beginning, almost out of hand. For one thing, he noted that, unlike Cypriot words, very *few* Linear B sign groups ended in the sign ⊔ (*se*), '-s', which suggested that 'Minoan' and Greek were not related. A logical enough deduction, and one that would trouble all subsequent decipherers including Ventris. Less logical was that Evans simply could not accept that the Minoans spoke and wrote an archaic form of Greek, which they took with them to Cyprus. In Evans's view, it was Minos and the Minoans, *not* the mainland Greeks, who ruled the roost: the 'Minoan' language could not possibly be Greek. He dismissed the similarity of the Linear B and Cypriot signs in the case of 'polo' as a mere coincidence of the kind that, in fairness to Evans, must be admitted to be only too misleadingly common in historical linguistics and decipherment. It is a general rule of decipherment that to allot sound values to unknown signs purely on their visual resemblance to known signs is a risky procedure, likely to be wrong.

Of course, this left the big question wide open: what was the language spoken by the Minoans, if it was not Greek? Ventris decided that it must be related to one of the languages known to have been spoken around the Aegean in the second millennium B.C., which included the three Anatolian languages Lydian, Carian and Lycian – and also Etruscan. Although Etruscan was spoken only in Italy during classical times and eventually disappeared altogether with the rise of Latin, the language was said by Herodotus originally to have been the language of an Anatolian people from Lydia who had migrated through the Aegean to Italy in pre-Greek times, presumably in the second millennium. Some archaeological support for this legend came from a 6th-century-B.C. stone inscription found on the island of Limnos, near Anatolia, in the 19th century, which appeared to be written in a language similar to Etruscan. (Modern scholars, it should be said, disagree with Herodotus and treat the Etruscans as indigenous to Italy; and they regard the Limnos inscription as a controversial enigma.)

The principal reason why Ventris favoured Etruscan over the three Anatolian languages came from his acceptance of the Evans theory that the Cypriot syllabary provided a key to Linear B and its 'Minoan' language. He noted that the Cypriot syllabary did not represent the consonants b, g and d, and proposed that the same was true of the 'Minoan' language. He further noted the very same feature in Etruscan, but *not* in the Anatolian languages. Therefore, 'Minoan' must be closely related to Etruscan. Pursuing this theory, he then allotted Cypriot sound values to many Linear B sign groups which he believed to be names – on the assumption that similar-looking signs in Cypriot and Linear B had similar values – and, hey presto, some Etruscan-sounding names, such as *Vilie* (compare Etruscan *Velia*) popped out of the tablets from Knossos! 'That we should find this typically Etruscan name used by the women of Minoan Crete...is a startling demonstration of the fundamental linguistic unity', Ventris audaciously claimed.

He was building a house of cards on shifting sands. Yet it is worth asking why he remained so committed to the Etruscan hypothesis – and so opposed to the Greek hypothesis – from 1940 right up to 1952. There were some solid reasons, such as Evans's arguments against Greek, the undoubted existence of pre-Greek inscriptions in the Aegean area, the

	Etruscan	Latin	Greek	Sanskrit
father	apa	pater	pater	pita
mother	ati	mater	mater, miter	mata
son	clan	filius	hyios	sunuh
daughter	sech	filia	thygater	duhita
wife	puia	mulier, femina, uxor	gyne	gna
brother	ruva	frater	(phrater)	bhrata
one	thu	oinos, unus	oine	e(kah)
two	zal	duo	dyo	dva
three	ci	tres	treis	trayah
four	sa	quattuor	tettares	catvarah
five	mach	quinque	pente	panca
six	huth	sex	hex	sat (sas)
ten	sar	decem	deka	dasa

The Etruscan script (opposite) is essentially the Greek alphabet, but Etruscan is not an Indo-European language (above).

Etruscan alphabet	Phonetic value	Greek alphabet	Phonetic value
A	*a*	AA	*a*
		B	*b*
) ⊃	*c (=k)*	<C	*g*
		D▷	*d*
ⱻⱻ	*e*	ⱻE	*e*
ꟻꟻ	*v*	F	*w*
I Ⱶ	*z (=ts)*	I	*z*
日目⊘	*h*	日H	*h*
⊗⊙○	*θ (=th)*	⊗⊕⊙	*th*
I	*i*	I	*i*
ꓘ	*k*	K	*k*
⅃	*l*	⅃	*l*
ꟽ Ⱞ	*m*	ꟽⰮꟽ	*m*
ꟼ ꟼ	*n*	ꟼN	*n*
⊞	*s*	X	*x*
		O	*o*
ꟼ ꟼ	*p*	⌐⌐	*p*
Ⱞ	*ś*	Ⱞ (?)	*s*
Ⴑ	*q*	Ⴑ	*q*
ꟼ Ⴃ	*r*	P	*r*
≀ ≀	*s*	Ʂ	*s*
T Ꞁ	*t*	T	*t*
Y V	*u, w*	ꝡYV	*u*
X	*ś*		
Φ Φ	*φ (=ph)*	ΦΦ	*ph*
Ψ Ψ	*χ (=kh)*	ΨΨ	*kh*
8	*f*		

various words in the ancient Greek language which the Greeks themselves knew to be 'barbarian' imports, and the evidence of Homer,
Herodotus and other commentators for the existence of pre-Greek (non-
Indo-European) languages in the Aegean. But over and above these,
Ventris seems to have set his heart on a non-classical, non-Indo-European linguistic solution to 'Minoan' because he disliked the dominance
of the classical languages over western culture. After the war, he even
wrote: 'Our researches have been prejudiced by conscious or unconscious
acceptance of the official Nazi doctrine, according to which all admirable
civilizations are due to Nordic blood (or at least to the speakers of Indo-
European languages), and which incidentally saw in the Etruscans an
earlier prototype of all those non-Aryan vices of luxury, obscenity, cruelty,
necromancy and usury for which the Jews were later to be scapegoats.' At
bottom, it would seem, Ventris's commitment to the Etruscan solution –
like that of Evans to 'his' Minoans – was emotional, not intellectual.

Something still more profound, even unfathomable, may have been
at stake for him here. For the tragic fact is, that while he was in the very
midst of writing his article, his mother Dorothea took an overdose of
barbitone and died on 16 June, while staying in a seaside hotel in north
Wales. The coroner's verdict was 'suicide while the balance of her mind
was disturbed'. Apparently, her personal anxieties, which she had confessed to Breuer not long before, combined with the stress on her Polish
family of a barbaric invasion, had finally proved too much for this sensitive, isolated woman.

Ventris never spoke of what happened to his mother – presumably it
was too painful to put into mere words – and never talked of either her or
his father, even to his closest friends. That summer he deserted the Highpoint flat and went to stay for a while with Gabo, who had now moved to
St Ives, the artists' colony on the Cornish coast, where Michael quietly
retreated into solitary work on his article. Returning to London and his
architectural course, he moved into a boarding house in Hampstead, and

did not go back to Highpoint, alone, until early October 1940, almost a month after the first German bombs fell on London.

From the flat he told Gabo and his wife in a long letter: 'I haven't written to you since the Blitz really started, so I thought maybe you'd be wondering whether I'm still alive.... [The raids] haven't bothered me much, though. It is the AA [anti-aircraft] fire which is the most disturbing.... In Hampstead we were near the railway line, and so they aimed around us most of the time. Several bombs fell very near, and we had some windows broken. Up here it is quieter, but whenever the shrapnel comes down on the six inches of concrete which lies between me and the open sky, it gives a resounding *dongggg*, which would no doubt wake me up if it happened while I was asleep.' Talking of the Minoan article, he explained what it was about, and that he had sent it to a journal, and then he added: 'I shan't spend much more time on it, but will concentrate purely on architecture from now on.'

In reality, from now on, Ventris would pursue his twin passions – architecture and the Minoan scripts – for the rest of his life. Although the first would feed the second, there was undoubtedly a rivalry between them: whenever he tried to give up his Minoan study, as he did several times, Linear B would reclaim him and take him away from architecture. In the end, the tension became a conflict that he was never able to resolve.

Thus, in July 1941, he wrote to his former headmaster Roxburgh. He was getting on quite well at the Architectural Association School, he said, and would soon be taking some intermediate exams of the Royal Institute of British Architects. But at the same time he enclosed his published article and requested a reference from Roxburgh for a specialist philological library. 'How the article got accepted is still a mystery to me.... I'm still working a bit on similar lines, and that's what I badly want to get into this library for.... I don't expect to be called up till some time next year.'

At Highpoint, he continued to live alone, surrounded by the Breuer furniture and the Picasso paintings and Gabo and Moore sculptures that he had inherited from his mother. Fellow students at the AA would come to see the famous modern flat and sometimes stay over. One of them, Graeme Shankland, later a well-known town planner, recalled that in the small but elegant kitchen there was sometimes visible 'a pile of unwashed dishes going up to the ceiling! Michael wasn't a very domesticated sort of person. He found that side of things rather a bore; he couldn't be concerned with it.'

Then, quite suddenly, he fell in love. Lois Knox-Niven, a couple of years older than Ventris (she entered the AA the year before him, in 1939), was 'a real knock-out', according to more than one of her student contemporaries. Her English cavalry officer father had died in 1923, when Lois was only three, from the effects of being gassed in the first world war, and her well-to-do Canadian mother had married again, this time to a wealthy former Coldstream Guards officer with a passion for flying and yachting who was chairman of the de Havilland Aircraft Co. Throughout the 1920s and after, he raced light aeroplanes, often accompanied by his new wife, who was also an able pilot, and flew in many parts of the world. (His obituary in *The Times* noted that he 'did as much as anybody to popularize the light aeroplane.') As a child, Lois seems to have been left to her own devices and formed a passion for animals as a substitute for her absent parents – at least that is what she herself felt about her childhood. In the later 1930s, as a young woman, she was sent to Vienna University and the Sorbonne in Paris to be 'finished', during which time she picked up some French and German, and practiced her skiing – though she never reached the Olympic standard of her glamorous mother. She also studied fine art and architecture; and this seems to have been what made her decide to train as an architect, against family precedent. It would be architecture that would be her strongest bond with Michael Ventris.

In wartime conditions, relationships developed quickly. The 19-year-old Ventris told Gabo in early 1942: 'It looks as if, in the ordinary way, we'll have a baby some time round next November – at least Betts [Lois]

Ventris (third from right) with fellow RAF trainees, 1943.

has changed her mind, and she wants to have it, and I don't think either that it would be quite right to stop new life when this world needs it so, quite apart from the risk. But the social politics of it is all rather involved, and we're in the process of working that out. So we *might* get clandestinely married – but all this is confidential in the extreme!' In the event, he and Lois married at a London registry office in April 1942 with two hired witnesses and no public announcement. Once again, Ventris had decided to ignore convention.

In a matter of months they were parted. In August, he was finally called up and joined the Royal Air Force for training as a pilot. Within a day or two of leaving Highpoint and his pregnant wife, he found himself in a tent in a field in Shropshire, his days filled with the menial activities of service life for a new conscript, living in close proximity to men with whom he had little in common. It must have been tough for him, and for his wife, but he took it fairly philosophically, judging from the long and frequent letters he wrote to Lois.

'A nice thing about camp is the way everyone gets talking to everyone else. Of course there are a number of people who are completely empty, and others whose charm doesn't rely on serious conversation. But all the same during meals, and when washing, and in the "shithouse", one gets a passing acquaintance with a great range of people.'

'Living under discipline, I begin to think, makes one sentimental – not quite in the modern sense of it, but more the late 18th-century one, like the *Sentimental Journey. –* A great increase in the amount of emotion that gets called up inside one by any small incidents and situations which show people in a sympathetic way – and a greater feeling for the charm of scenes and landscape. I'm afraid I shall become a Betjeman if discipline continues, and modern architecture will be got back to as something rather unusual, and, if I am not careful, unfelt!'

He was determined not to stagnate in the RAF. Besides a great deal of reading on a wide range of subjects, including politics and science, and frequent visits to the movies, he worked at picking up five or more European languages (his letters to Gabo were soon entirely in Russian); he made endless sketches of aircraft and buildings, including a constantly remodelled house for himself, Lois and children; and, off and on, he thought about Linear B.

It was something of a coup to receive a letter in late 1942 from Evans's long-time friend and now executor, (Sir) John Myres, the retired professor of ancient history at Oxford, appreciating his 1940 article in the *American Journal of Archaeology.* Following Evans's death in 1941, Myres was trying to prepare for publication well over 1500 Minoan tablets, for the vast majority had been kept by Evans to himself. Ventris told his wife (one of his rare references to Linear B in their correspondence; she did not share his fascination): 'I hope he'll let me know how his researches are going, as he's got much more material to work on, and he's a big shot, and he's very cautious, so whatever he establishes should be pretty *echt*. But I'm afraid it'll rather shake him to find I wrote the opus at 17 – I mentioned it [in reply] half out of conceit and half out of thinking the whole thing was rather a joke anyway.' To Myres himself, he wrote enthusiastically about the great man's plans to publish all the tablets: 'I doubt if I'll have the leisure to be tempted into reattacking them. But it will give opportunity for a wide circle of researchers to get to work and progress should pick up speed.' Then he concluded rather presciently: 'At present one can remain sure that no Champollion is working quietly in a corner and preparing a full and startling revelation, as no one has access to sufficient reproductions.' After the war, young Ventris-Champollion and old Sir John Myres would have a lot to do with each other.

Meanwhile, his RAF training was taking him away from being a pilot and towards being a navigator. Pilots enjoyed more prestige, and no doubt his wife's family, as keen fliers, looked down on navigation; but Ventris had been drawn to maps and map-making since school, and liked the mathematical, intellectual aspect of navigation. Although he flew solo a few times during his training, he did not feel confident as a pilot. Perhaps he disliked having to react quickly, as a pilot must, and preferred to have time, as a navigator has, to consider alternative courses of action. As an architect, in a somewhat similar way, he would always prefer thoughtful analysis to the more spontaneous creative aspects of design. At any rate, in mid-1943, he was sent to Canada for further navigational training, leaving behind Lois and the infant Nikki, who had arrived in early December ('the nicest present St Nicholas ever brought'), and for whom the Ventrises asked Naum Gabo to be a godfather and Ben Nicholson to paint an abstract nursery picture.

'From the air Manitoba looks like an immense Ben – a regular checkerboard of russet, ruddy-grey, green and black divided by N–S and E–W roads,' Michael airgraphed to Lois. 'On Main Street [in Winnipeg] at night you hear more Polish and Ukrainian spoken than English, which is rather intriguing.' Food, too, was plentiful and excellent in Canada.

Then it was back to cramped, rationed, wartime England, now as an officer qualified to navigate bombers. He joined a squadron based at Holme, not far from York, and flew Halifaxes over Germany from

November 1944 to April 1945. Although the Luftwaffe was no longer the power it had been, this was still dangerous work. For example, he recorded a mission to attack Worms, in a private diary begun in February 1945: 'I am afraid we have demolished or battered the cathedral at Worms. Of course all the sights are lost to me in my little office...because I am so preoccupied over our exact position: but apparently there was quite a lot to see, and though it didn't menace us particularly closely, the defence was pretty versatile – fairly heavy flak, fighter flares, rockets and scare-crows.... But still we were surprised on getting back to find that ten kites were missing from the Group.... There are so many causes for an aircraft to go missing, and the enemy is only responsible for a bare half of them: collisions, being bombed from above, engine failures, and landings in poor weather are things that one is not particularly worried by, though one should be.' According to *The Bomber Command War Diaries*, out of 324 bombers on this particular raid (21–22 February 1945), 10 Halifaxes and 1 Lancaster were lost, while 64 per cent of Worms was destroyed or

Ventris's Christmas card to his wife Lois, Germany, 1945.

damaged, 239 people were killed and 35,000 were bombed out, from a population of approximately 58,000.

The end of the war in Europe was not the end of war service for Ventris. But he managed to avoid being sent out East by volunteering to go to Germany, where an ability to speak German was in demand among the victorious Allies and in the soon-to-be-established Control Commission. Based at Plön, north of Hamburg, at first he was quite interested in the work, which included analysing the structure of the Gestapo in Kiel, taking German prisoners to Copenhagen and attempts at liaison with the Russians; but as 1946 dawned without any prospect of his demobilization, he felt depressed and full of self-doubt about his future life. He became more and more anxious to return to London and his interrupted architectural training. His visit to Copenhagen, with its plethora of 'vernacular' modern buildings (in stark contrast to London), had been an eye-opener. As an exercise, in late 1945 he designed an officer's mess at Plön and admitted to his wife: 'I'm all for reducing the thing to a detailed system (perhaps because I find great pain and difficulty in designing) and providing oneself with readymade questionnaires to fill up on all the points that require research' – a hint of his future direction as an architect and as a decipherer.

Linear B had now reappeared on the horizon, after a longish gap, in the shape of a letter from Myres offering to show him all the unpublished tablets. Ventris expressed enthusiasm to visit him – just as soon as he could escape from the Control Commission.

At last, in the late summer of 1946, he was released. He could go back to Highpoint, to his wife and two children (a daughter, Tessa, had arrived in April that year), to the Architectural Association School – and to Linear B. One of the first things he did on his return in August was to take a train to Oxford to meet Myres and see the Knossos tablets for himself.

3
Embryo Architect

'It is the privilege of individual genius to follow no system beyond a creative intuition; but in group working some minimum of method is essential.'

Michael Ventris, 'Group Working', in *Plan* (journal of the Architectural Students Association), 1948

During the two years or so after he was demobbed, Linear B took a back seat in Ventris's life, although he never stopped working at it. In 1946–48, he threw himself into his architectural training at the AA, which had been interrupted in 1942, determined and happy to make up for time lost during the war. The methods of design he would evolve in this period would later prove useful in decipherment too.

Immediately after the war, the Architectural Association School, now back at its Bedford Square premises in central London, was an exciting place to study, its students bubbling with modern aesthetic and social ideas and ideals, aware of the potential of recent developments in constructional materials and technologies, and hopeful of finding much new and interesting work in post-war reconstruction under the Labour government. Before the war there had been 250 students at the school, now there were 450. As a result, Ventris found himself doing drawings in a Nissen hut in a freezing cold winter. Nevertheless, he was soon working day and night.

'At that time we were all rabid socialists...and one of us was a member of the Communist Party,' Oliver Cox, who was closest to Ventris at the AA, recalled in the 1980s. 'Michael's theories about design showed a development of analytical approach which today you would describe as Marxist. And it wouldn't have disturbed Michael at all for anyone to say to him: "I see you're a Marxist." He'd say: "Well, what of it?" He wouldn't regard it as important.' Certainly, Michael and Lois chose Labour at their first opportunity to vote: the landslide general election of 1945 that threw out the Churchill government – against the instinctive Conservatism of his wife's family.

He, Lois, Cox and Graeme Shankland – who had all been at the school in Hadley Common at the start of the war – instantly formed a close group within the 1946 intake. Together, occasionally with input from others, they collaborated on a wide range of student projects. They designed a block of flats, a multi-storey garage, an arts centre, a factory for Penguin Books – for which they were briefed by the 'King Penguin' himself, the founder Allen Lane – and an opera house. In addition, Cox, Ventris and another architect entered a professional competition to design a London headquarters for the Trades Union Congress; although they did not win, their design was published in the *Architects' Journal*. Ventris found the problem of designing the opera house and TUC auditoria a particularly fascinating challenge, because both spaces entailed complex geometry and calculation to ensure that the opera house stage was clearly visible to 2000 spectators (some of them in boxes) and that individual trade unionists standing in their places could be heard throughout the congress hall. (At this time, pre-transistors, public address systems were primitive.) Most of the precise, highly detailed drawings the group produced, with Ventris's immaculate, almost print-like hand lettering, are preserved.

'Group working' was then something of a buzz phrase among architecture students – in contrast to the typical hierarchy among architects in the profession in which specialists worked in a firm under the general direction of one commanding figure, who might well be a prima donna like Le Corbusier. To a considerable extent, the 'group working' concept was being forced on an unprepared post-war profession by the advent of multifarious and increasingly complex materials and construction techniques, which required greater interaction between architects on a project than was necessary in designing a more traditional building. But for the Cox/Shankland/Ventris partnership, group working was almost an article of faith, and also chimed with the socialist ethos of the time. 'Like the architects of the Restoration and the engineers of the Industrial Revolution for whom he had an intense admiration, he was an ardent anti-specialist,' wrote a *Times* obituarist of Shankland in 1984. 'The "inter-professional team" was no catchword to him, it was the way he worked throughout his whole professional life.' Cox and Ventris took the same view.

Thus, in 1948, in the wake of the limited success of a group in designing an icon of the age – the new United Nations building in New York, Ventris published a conversation between architects about group working in *Plan*, a new student magazine of the AA. The views expressed about it were rather mixed. Perhaps the most original contribution was Ventris's own, a kind of manifesto for his method of architectural design, and also (though naturally he did not mention it) for his future approach to decipherment.

'It is the privilege of individual genius to follow no system beyond a creative intuition; but in group working some minimum of method is essential,' he wrote. 'Equally unsatisfactory is the lazy partner who cannot get anything down on paper beyond the 3B envelope doodle, and the keen one whose splendid sketches lie around to get filthy, are mutilated at every handling, and finally cannot be found. If some disciplining of the routine part of the design process is essential to producing a group scheme, it is equally valuable, in making one's private work less of a headache. There are three golden rules:

1   Put down conceitedly every requirement, argument, inspiration and mind's eye picture that occurs during the design process, and put it down as concisely, enthusiastically and *pictorially* as possible.
2   Phrase your conclusions, set out and colour your pictures, in such a way that they will mean the most to you (or to a colleague), at a second reading.
3   File everything where you will still find it fresh and clean tomorrow or in a year's time. Architecture needs paper in order to take form: enjoy and respect your material.'

Maybe this does not sound revolutionary, but it was undoubtedly very unusual in architecture at a time when architects generally thought of themselves more as ('long-haired') artists than as analysts or scientists. Ventris's method attempted to pinion the butterfly of the imagination, so that each part was clearly displayed and open to critique by colleagues and, if necessary, modification. The catch was, as Ventris himself admitted later in the article, that 'logic alone' is not enough to produce architecture. It would not be enough to decipher Linear B, either. But whereas in decipherment, Ventris's imagination could take wing from its logical foundations, for some reason in architecture it would generally remain earthbound.

His personal encounter with Le Corbusier illustrates the point nicely. In 1947, during the centenary of the Architectural Association, the student committee at the school (which included Cox and Ventris) invited 'Corb' to visit, and rather to their surprise he accepted. He arrived, and the students gathered round, and at some point Ventris explained to Le Corbusier the nuances of a simple machine he had been steadily refining since his work on the officer's mess in Germany, called the Perspector or Perspectron, by means of which architects could get coordinate dimensions for drawing perspectives. When he had finished,

Le Corbusier responded by simply dismissing the need for such calculations. To draw an interior perspective, 'Corb' said (according to a listening Cox), he put the vanishing point for the right walls over on the left and the vanishing point for the left walls on the right, 'and then I get the impression that I'm *in* the place. I've got no time for these camera views of an interior.' Regardless, an unfazed Ventris, with the help of Cox, took out a patent on the machine, which turned out to be a clever precursor of the current digital computerized perspective drawing systems.

Ventris would have been right at home with these, had he lived longer. But one feels he would probably never have overcome his limitations as an artist. Oliver Cox, a skilled painter whose son is a professional artist and illustrator, knew that Ventris was frustrated even when a student at the AA. 'I irritated him immensely, for I had a facility for freehand drawing and Michael desperately wanted to know how to free up. Being a great intellectual, the brain was dominating whatever he did. Yet as your hand draws, there must be a sensuous pleasure in doing that creative thing. He had the desire to create, to draw freely, but his intellectual powers held his hand in restraint. He was always wanting correct perspectives.... One of his philosophies was: never throw away a doodle. But, of course, it makes a difference if your doodles are immaculate and inhibited!' (Ventris even had trouble designing a purely fantastic 'mobile' for his baby son, telling his wife, significantly: 'I feel one does better starting from actual objects than getting an idea in vacuo.')

One cannot help wondering about his artistic inhibition, given Ventris's truly exceptional linguistic gifts. Why should someone who was able to express himself in words freely in ten or more languages be unable to liberate his lines on a page? Obviously it helped him greatly that he had learnt foreign languages as a child – whereas he came to drawing later. Also important, one feels from his work on Linear B, is that in languages Ventris could always be sure there were rules, limits, a right and a wrong way to say something, imposed by a particular language's grammatical structure and the usage of native speakers – unlike in painting and sculpture. Then there was his liking for functionalism and his dislike of decoration and embellishment: a certain coolness about sensuous pleasure, even a touch of puritanism (but without even a trace of conventional religious belief). Finally – although this is speculation – he seems to have had a fear of art. Ventris personally knew major artists, such as Gabo and Nicholson, as a teenager, and must have realized he was not one of them. He knew what had happened to his art-loving mother. Choosing architecture as his field was perhaps partly his way of controlling art, making it subservient to function, and of mastering his fear of losing control over his mind.

All his strengths and weaknesses came out on a group visit to Sweden (and Denmark) in the summer of 1947. Swedish architects had embraced modernism well before the second world war, and because of the country's neutrality in the war, it had not been bombed and so Sweden was ahead of other European countries (even Denmark) in building techniques and the organization of the architectural profession. Cox, Shankland and Ventris were hoping to get work in a Swedish design office when they went to live in Stockholm in June, and to imbibe some of the new knowledge not available to them in London.

Arriving in Sweden by boat, Cox and Shankland were startled to find Ventris speaking Swedish to the customs officers – he had given little previous sign of his language abilities. He had picked the language up from books in the couple of weeks before they departed. It quickly got him a job, though he told his wife (who joined them later) modestly: 'I've laid myself open by starting off in Swedish, with the result that nobody addresses me in English and half the time I haven't much of a clue. Everybody "du"s each other, which is a relief, and good mornings and goodbyes consist invariably of a shout of "hej!" or "hej hej!" or "hej på dig!".' He was amused to find the group's room in Stockholm reserved in the name of Wennquist.

Oliver :– " Has anyone seen the carrots? "

A cartoon by Oliver Cox, showing Ventris, Shankland and Cox in Stockholm, 1947.

His two friends were not so lucky, lacking any Swedish. They had to be content to be outsiders, touring Swedish buildings and workshops, while looking after the group's domestic arrangements and, in Cox's case, doing funny, slightly wry illustrations of their communal life to accompany Michael's letters, for the benefit of Lois and young Nikki. (Cox also told Lois: 'Graeme and I...have quite a job getting your news out of Michael.') Mostly, Ventris is pictured as the leader of the group.

One of the running jokes between them concerned 'sharawaggi'. As in the following comment from Michael to Lois describing his temporary job: 'At the moment I'm drawing out 1:50s of a remodelled Konsum shop.... The engineer comes along and suggests a little bit of "SKOJ" (fun, sharawaggi etc.) which I don't feel very well qualified to achieve.'

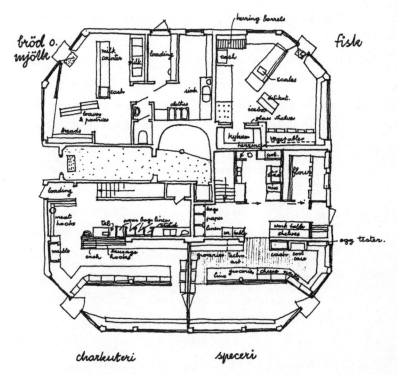

Konsum shops, an architectural sketch by Ventris, Stockholm, 1947.

Any request for 'sharawaggi', i.e. embellishment, would always bother him as an architect. Thus in his travels in and around Stockholm and in Copenhagen, among Ventris's many pages of notes and drawings on the constructional details of walls, doors, windows, roofs, light fittings and so on, and on the properties of materials – there is even a long note on the chemistry of different kinds of concrete and cement renderings – one comes across comments critical of embellishment like: 'Why, oh why, these boxed out windows in brick – pure drawingboardery!' and 'Hall is disappointing: bad woods on front doors. *Appalling* festoons up the side!'

Still, Ventris fell for modern Scandinavian architecture and would later give his own house in Hampstead a distinctly Scandinavian feel. His letters to his wife speak of the pleasures of life in Stockholm: sunny days and luminous northern nights, clean air, sea bathing, bicycling in and around the city looking at the buildings, lots of charming fair-haired children – and decent food ('Reindeer is off the ration, and it makes excellent sandwiches'). Once, they took a lift by car out of the city to see a modern villa, stopped on a rocky peninsula for lunch and a bathe, and on the way found themselves in a vast area of whortleberries and wild straw-berries; they promptly 'got down on their hands and knees like small boys'. It sounds a bit like a scene out of an early Bergman film.

In a polemical article written for *Plan*, 'Function and arabesque', on his return to the AA, Ventris called Sweden and Denmark an architec-tural 'paradise', certainly in comparison to the 'paradise lost' of England. He tried to encapsulate what English architects could learn from the Swedes and Danes, without mere copying, as in the neoclassical architec-ture of his old school Stowe. 'The enemy has always been the classical. At best, Roman motives have been but a light disguise masking a continuing native tradition. The columned building, antiquarian or monumental, insults its surroundings by its timeless irrelevance.' His conclusion was even more hard-hitting: 'As students now, the future looks black. There are too many of us, there are no jobs, travel is ended, reactionaries still top the profession, craftsmanship is dying, and the architect is unrespected. But if the visual order of England in the second half of the 20th century depends on anyone, it depends on you. If you can possibly afford it, don't give up architecture. Don't emigrate. Help regain that Paradise.'

In the summer of 1948, the group took the AA's final exams and they all passed out with honours. To celebrate the end of their training, they decided to make a last trip together. The Ventrises, being well off, acquired an old Ford army van. The idea was to take it across the Channel and drive through France to Switzerland and into Italy ending up in Rome, and then return via the south of France; to stop at interesting buildings wherever they could; and to camp as much as possible. Michael, who did not yet drive, was to act as navigator and interpreter: a role for which he was eminently suited. The two Ventris children were to be left in England with relatives.

It was a memorable journey for many reasons, which Oliver Cox recalled with nostalgia several decades later. Ventris's command of languages was at its most impressive in the Vatican City. They were keen to get into a part of it not open to the public, so Ventris went up to one of the Swiss Guards and talked to him for a quarter of an hour. When he came back, he said, 'Yes, they'll let us in here.' Then one of the guards shouted some question, just as the group was going in. Oliver asked Michael what the guard had said. 'He asked what part of Switzerland I came from.' He had been talking to the guard in fluent Swiss German, which he had first learnt as a child at school in Switzerland.

But the linguistic one-upmanship, however unboastful, could be a bit wearing too for the others; and it also had its funny side. Ventris's Italian was good, but not as good as his French and German (and his Russian). In Italy, he and Cox went out one day in search of paraffin for their camping stove. Ventris did not know the Italian word for it. In the shop they were offered 'petrolio', but they both decided it sounded so inflammable they could not risk trying it and producing an explosion. So they went to a chemist's shop and bought some very expensive liquid called 'paraffina'. Although Cox told Ventris that it looked so thick it might be medical paraffin meant for clearing the bowels, Ventris insisted and poured it into the stove. But it was the wrong stuff – and it would take them many hours to clean out the stove. 'It was one of the few incidents on any holiday when Michael was laughed at and humbled. He would always try to edge out of being in that position if he could. But he took it very well, because it was shared with me.... Most of us, especially the English, are quite good on holiday at being a bit of an ass. Poor old Michael didn't like that and always wanted to be on the side of the natives speaking the lingo.'

While in Italy, Ventris took the opportunity to do some research on the Etruscans – they drove through Tuscany – but of course he did not tell the rest of the group what he was up to. In fact, he was already mulling over in the privacy of his mind his next move in attacking Linear B, now that he was a qualified architect. Soon, Cox, Shankland and Lois discovered this in a somewhat unfortunate way, characteristic of Ventris. When they proposed driving to Marseilles to see Le Corbusier's famous block of flats, the Unité d'Habitation, which was under construction, and then taking a slow route back to England, Michael put his foot down and became obstinate. He said he had to get back quickly to meet someone in connection with Linear B research, and would not tell anyone, including his wife, why his appointment was so important. Somewhat grudgingly, they cut short a rather pleasant holiday and headed home; and as soon as they reached London and had unloaded the van, Ventris dashed off. 'He could just withdraw, go into his shell and be as happy as a sand-boy', remembered Cox. 'It was a marvellous castle, his brain. That is why he was happy and not at all affected if someone else was worried and upset for some reason.... He was not *quite* human, I sometimes think!'

Unknown, and perhaps incomprehensible to his architect circle (even if Michael had wanted to explain it), Sir John Myres and an important visitor from the United States, the formidable Linear B analyst, Alice Kober, were waiting for Ventris in Oxford in August 1948. Once again, the Linear B obsession was luring him away from architecture and conventional obligations.

4
Architect and Decipherer

*'I have good hopes that a sufficient number of people working on
these lines will before long enable a satisfactory solution to be found.
To them I offer my best wishes, being forced by pressure of other work
to make this my last small contribution to the problem.'*

Michael Ventris, *Mid-Century Report: The Languages of the Minoan
and Mycenaean Civilisations*, 1950

Sir John Myres and Ventris had been in touch ever since late 1942, when Ventris had just joined the RAF. The eminent old scholar perceived that this young architect, despite being an amateur in classics and archaeology, had an original mind and was deeply interested in the problem of Linear B – though he would never quite make Ventris out. Throughout, their relationship would be one of mutual but wary respect. In 1946, in Oxford, Myres had shown Ventris Evans's collection of tablets, tablet photographs and drawings, and notes from Knossos, and invited his help in publishing the collection. At that time Ventris was too busy with architecture, but by the first half of 1948, while he continued to beaver away on architectural projects at the AA, the two men were in constant communication about Linear B. Myres was full of praise for Ventris's sample-page drawings of some inscriptions; and the American scholar helping Myres, Alice Kober, observed aptly: 'Mr Ventris would have no trouble getting a job as scribe for King Minos'. By June, it was settled that Ventris – without payment, merely for the love of Linear B –

would spend much of August and the early autumn with Myres in Oxford, transcribing all the Knossos tablets for the Oxford University Press. 'I won't let you down,' he assured Sir John.

But he did. Having cut short his European trip, upsetting his wife and architect friends, and dashed to Oxford in late August to meet Myres and Kober, the next thing we know is that Ventris has pulled right out of the collaboration. 'Dear Sir John,' he wrote in a brief, hurried and exceptionally revealing letter headed 'Oxford Station, Monday night', 'You will probably think me quite mad if I try and account for the reasons why I'll be absent on Tuesday morning, and why I should like to ask either Miss Kober, or the other girl that you mentioned, to complete the transcription.' He continued: 'One would have thought that years in the Forces would have cured one of irrational and irresistible impulses of dread or homesickness. But however much I tell myself that I am a swine to let you down after all my glib promises and conceited preparations – I am hit at last by the overwhelming realization that I shall not be able to stand 6 weeks' work alone in Oxford, and that I am an idiot not to stick to my own last. Perhaps it's rather weakmindedness to throw up the sponge, than to grind on with something one's liable to make a botch job of – I don't know. In any case I shall await *Scripta Minoa* with great interest – and be too ashamed to look inside.'

What had gone wrong? It would be simple to say that Ventris and Myres (and Kober) did not hit it off – and this appears to have been the impression Ventris chose to give to his wife on return to Highpoint, which she passed on to Oliver Cox when he enquired what had happened at Michael's super-urgent Linear B meeting: 'he had a terrible row' (a highly unlikely scenario for a man as restrained as Ventris). No doubt there was a personality clash, but there was more to the incident than that. By 'stick to my own last', Ventris apparently meant 'stick to what I know professionally', i.e. architecture. 'Weakmindedness' is a further hint at the growing tension between his two passions. Strong words of self-criticism like 'mad', 'irrational', 'swine', 'glib', 'conceited', 'idiot' and 'ashamed' – strong at least by Ventris's unemotional standards – suggest a mind in turmoil. He would write in this fevered tone only once again in his life, just before his death.

Yet of course there *was* a genuine scholarly disagreement. Three years after the incident, Ventris told a fellow decipherer, Emmett Bennett Jr, that he had backed out of Myres's publication 'largely because I felt the whole project was a bit out of hand and I didn't have enough knowledge or "personality" to get it improved.'

To understand properly what was at stake, we need to go back ten years, to the last few years of Evans's life. Notwithstanding his great four-volume publication, *The Palace of Minos* – with regard to the Minoan script, Evans left a disorganized legacy. In 1909, he had published (with Oxford University Press) *Scripta Minoa*, but this contained the two other scripts discovered in Crete, the Hieroglyphic and Linear A, hardly any Linear B tablets. Of the more than 3000 Linear B tablets and fragments (there were about 1600 tablets) excavated by Evans and others at Knossos, only two or three hundred had been published by 1941, the year of Evans's death, most of them only in the 1930s, along with a sign list seriously flawed by Evans's falling for the pictographic fallacy mentioned in chapter 1 (many of the signs he had read as pictograms/logograms were really phonetic signs). The arduous task of completing their publication now fell to Myres, who was already well into his seventies. He would labour at *Scripta Minoa*, volume 2, for ten years with fading eyesight and help from a few others, chiefly Kober and Bennett, but he was in an impossible position: trapped between a loyal desire to keep faith with the faulty sign list prepared by Evans and the clear perception of Kober, Bennett and Ventris that a more logical, scientific approach to classifying the signs was required.

There was also the startling fact that more Linear B tablets had recently been discovered, this time not in Crete but in mainland Greece, in the western Peloponnese. In 1939, the American archaeologist Carl Blegen, having completed a famous dig at Troy, had struck lucky with his first trial trench at a place he believed to be the site of ancient Pylos, the city made famous in Homer's *Iliad* as the seat of King Nestor. The result was almost 600 new pieces of Linear B – and a serious embarrassment to the Evans theory that Linear B was exclusively the writing of the Minoans. For if this were so, what were Linear B tablets doing in large quantity in mainland Greece? The 88-year-old Evans did not respond to Blegen's find, but his followers rapidly came up with explanations, such as that the tablets at Pylos were 'loot from Crete' or that an illiterate Greek ruler had raided Minoan Crete and carried off its scribes to work in his own palace at Pylos. Whatever proved to be the truth, Blegen's discovery was bound to have a profound effect on all scholars working on the decipherment of Linear B.

There was just time before the second world war intervened for the new pieces to be cleaned, mended and photographed, and then deposited in the Bank of Athens, where they remained intact during the next few turbulent years. The photographs were taken to the United States on the last American ship to leave the Mediterranean in 1940, after Italy declared war. Blegen entrusted their analysis to Bennett, his doctoral student at the University of Cincinnati, but he could get down to the task only after doing his war service as a cryptanalyst.

Throughout the 1940s, therefore, the situation for active research on Linear B – as opposed to scholarly speculation – was complicated and unsatisfactory. The tablets themselves were mostly inaccessible, in storage in Athens and Crete. Not very clear photographs and probably somewhat inaccurate drawings by Evans were under scrutiny in Britain and America by Myres, Ventris, Kober and Bennett, at first independently of each other (though keeping in touch by correspondence). Myres in Oxford was examining the entire set of Knossos tablets, but not those from Pylos, and would not publish them in *Scripta Minoa*, volume 2, until 1952; Ventris in London could work only with the few tablets published by Evans and others; ditto Kober in New York, until she began to help Myres in 1947; Bennett at Cincinnati and then Yale University had the Pylos archive, but comparatively little access to the Knossos tablets, which were obviously essential for comparison in compiling a definitive Linear B sign list. (Eventually, in 1949, Bennett was shown the Knossos tablets, in exchange for showing the Pylos tablets to Kober.) Overall, the situation was a mess, though not a hopeless one.

Nevertheless, during this time, both Bennett and Kober were able to carry out analyses that would be as vital to Ventris as the ground-breaking work of earlier scholars of the ancient Egyptian script (especially Thomas Young) had been to Champollion in deciphering the hieroglyphs. But their analyses were different in kind. Bennett's work may be likened to clearing the terrain of jungle and straightening the path; Kober's was more in the nature of proposing a methodology that would enable the decipherment to move forwards along a path of progress.

First, Bennett proved that while the numerical systems of Linear A and Linear B were very similar, the systems of measurement were not. Linear A has a system of fractional signs, e.g. ½, ⅔, ¾, while Linear B records fractional quantities in terms of smaller units, like pounds and pence or feet and inches. Besides being useful information, this added further weight to the suspicion that Linear B represented a language different from that of Linear A – probably from outside Crete since Linear B had been found in mainland Greece, unlike Linear A. (Evans had of course believed that both scripts wrote 'Minoan' – a view shared by Myres and Ventris, but not by Bennett and Kober, during the 1940s.)

More important, though, was Bennett's wrestling with the thousands of text characters in the Pylos tablets, to produce a sign list in which some 89 signs – presumably (but not yet provably) phonetic in function – were logically distinguished from each other. To do this, he had to identify *allographs* (equivalents) of the same sign, e.g. 'a' and 'ɑ', 'k' and 'ʀ', 's' and 'ʂ', if we take the roman script, and also the same sign written by two and more different scribal hands, i.e. handwriting discrepancies. When we know what the signs and sign groups mean in a language, such identification is quite easy, even if we are sometimes foxed by someone's illegible handwriting. Imagine, though, that you have to read some hand-written, and possibly semi-scribbled text in an unknown script and language – how would you know that the sign group 'ask' was the same word as '*ask*'? In addition, Bennett had to find ways to distinguish the 89 ?phonetic signs from a second class of signs, pictographic/iconic, which were apparently used as logograms (for instance, signs such as 🜊 and ⛩ on page 25). Evans and others had already done this, but there was absolutely no guarantee they were correct in their identications. By dint of careful analysis, Bennett managed to classify correctly signs such as the 'double-axe', 𐘂, and 'throne-and-sceptre', 𐙈, – which might have been thought to be logograms from their appearance – among the 89 ?phonetic signs, *not* among the logograms.

Besides painstaking visual comparisons of endless sign forms, Bennett achieved his sorting largely by using two techniques. One was a laborious comparison of the *contexts* of all the characters on the tablets; for example a lone sign which occurred only with numerals and was clearly iconic was almost certainly a logogram. (You could easily guess that '£' or '$' were logograms from a long list of goods with their prices.) The other technique involved frequency analysis of signs and sign combinations – counts of how frequent or infrequent each sign was, both in itself and in combination with other signs, and also in relation to its position within sign groups – which we shall discuss properly later in connection with Ventris's use of the same statistical technique. To give just one example here, Bennett calculated that the 'double-axe' and 'throne-and-sceptre' signs were very frequent signs in the Pylos tablets, often found at the beginning of sign groups but also regularly found within sign groups, and seldom found alone like the obvious logograms. If the two signs really were logograms (or determinatives) with some kind of religious or royal significance, as Evans suspected, their high frequency would suggest an unusually large number of persons at Pylos possessing religious or royal honours. And even if one accepted this explanation for the occurrence of the signs at the *beginning* of sign groups (where a priest's or ruler's designation would naturally go), how would one explain their occurrence *within* sign groups? Thus Bennett ruled in favour of the two signs being more likely to be phonetic than logographic, though he could not entirely exclude the possibility that they could act as logograms at the beginning of sign groups but as phonetic signs within sign groups.

'How difficult the task is only those who have tried can tell', wrote John Chadwick of Bennett's sign list compilation in *The Decipherment of Linear B*. Ventris was so impressed with it that he immediately adopted it for his own work, instead of Myres's idiosyncratic sign list. Furthermore, Bennett's conclusion that there were 89 signs in the list, rather than a much smaller number between 20 and 40, meant that the Linear B script probably was basically a syllabary, and definitely not an alphabet. (The English alphabet, with 26 letters, has ten fewer letters than the Russian alphabet, and four more than the Hebrew alphabet; syllabaries have upwards of 40 signs – 46 in Japanese *kana*, 56 in the Cypriot script, as discussed in chapter 2.)

If Bennett was dedicated, the somewhat older Kober, one senses, was driven; and it is hard to write about her without a certain pathos, for she died of cancer in 1950 at the age of only 43, a mere two years before Ventris announced his decipherment. It seems reasonable to compare her with Rosalind Franklin, the unlucky competitor of Crick and Watson in the DNA story (who died young and probably missed sharing their Nobel prize), for Kober was theoretically well placed to have 'cracked' Linear B, besides sharing Franklin's caution and determination (even obstinacy). However, on the evidence of Kober's published work, it seems doubtful she would have succeeded, as we shall now see.

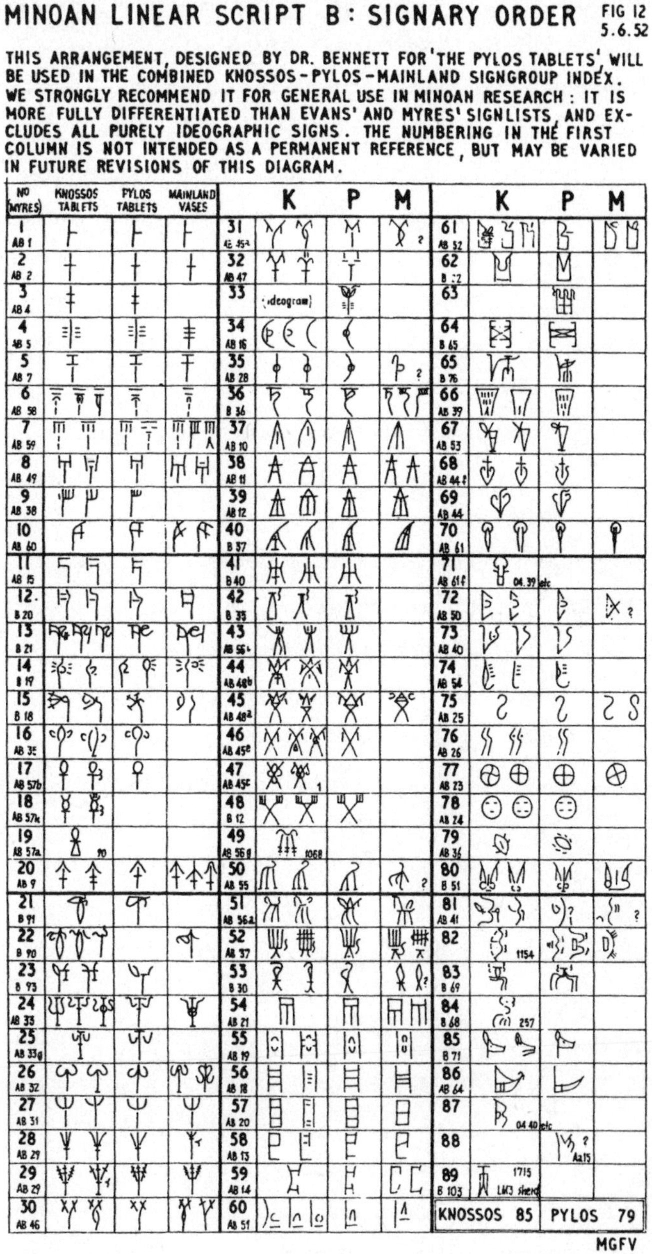
MINOAN LINEAR SCRIPT B : SIGNARY ORDER
FIG 12 5.6.52
THIS ARRANGEMENT, DESIGNED BY DR. BENNETT FOR 'THE PYLOS TABLETS', WILL BE USED IN THE COMBINED KNOSSOS-PYLOS-MAINLAND SIGNGROUP INDEX. WE STRONGLY RECOMMEND IT FOR GENERAL USE IN MINOAN RESEARCH : IT IS MORE FULLY DIFFERENTIATED THAN EVANS' AND MYRES' SIGNLISTS, AND EXCLUDES ALL PURELY IDEOGRAPHIC SIGNS. THE NUMBERING IN THE FIRST COLUMN IS NOT INTENDED AS A PERMANENT REFERENCE, BUT MAY BE VARIED IN FUTURE REVISIONS OF THIS DIAGRAM.
NO (MYRES)
KNOSSOS TABLETS
PYLOS TABLETS
MAINLAND VASES
K P M
K P M
(ideogram)
KNOSSOS 85
PYLOS 79
MGFV

Ventris's drawing of Emmett Bennett Jr's Linear B signary.

Superficially, her career was that of a typical classicist of her time. She studied Latin and Greek and took a PhD from Columbia University with a dissertation on 'Color terms in the Greek poets', then she began teaching at a college. But as Bennett wrote after her death, in her mid-twenties Kober had developed a 'consuming interest' in the undeciphered scripts of Crete. It would do her academic status no good (ditto for Bennett), yet as soon as she could, she set about learning as many ancient languages as possible, chiefly in order to be able to eliminate them as candidates for the languages of Linear A and B, while also studying archaeology in the field – in New Mexico and Greece – and, even more determinedly, mathematics (for its use in statistics) and physics and chemistry (for their methodology). Everything, including marriage, was sacrificed to her pursuit of the Minoan scripts.

The result was a series of important, ruthlessly logical papers on the Cretan scripts published between 1943 and her early death, notably in the *American Journal of Archaeology*. (Not surprisingly, she firmly ignored Ventris's speculative, 'Etruscan', 1940 paper in the same journal.) Their distinctive feature was Kober's conviction that with enough material available, there was no absolute need for a bilingual inscription like the Rosetta stone: it should be possible, simply by an intelligent search for *patterns* in the unknown Linear B characters, to determine the nature of the 'Minoan' script and its language, and hence, if the language was in fact related to a known language, to decipher Linear B.

Her most important practical contribution to the decipherment came from a suggestion originally made by Evans: that there was evidence of inflection (declension and conjugation) in Linear B. She took it up in a paper, 'Inflection in Linear Class B', published in the *AJA* in 1946. Kober was of course familiar with declension in Latin and Greek, where nouns are inflected according to their number (singular/plural/dual) and gender (masculine/feminine/neuter), and their case (nominative/accusative/ genitive/dative, e.g. domin**us**/domin**um**/domin**i**/domin**o**), and verbs are

inflected as they conjugate (e.g. am**o**/am**as**/am**at**/am**amus**/am**atis**/
am**ant**). There is relatively little declension/conjugation in English (e.g.
potato/potato**es** or the Latin-derived hippopotam**us**/hippopotam**i**, I
love/she love**s**/they love), more in French (e.g. j'aim**e**/tu aim**es**/il aim**e**/
nous aim**ons**/vous aim**ez**/ils aim**ent**). In Linear B, Kober identified five
groups of words taken from various published Knossos tablets, with three
words in each group – dubbed 'Kober's triplets' by a slightly teasing
Ventris – which suggested to her the presence of declension. She could
not know what the words meant, but their contexts in the tablets seemed
to be the same, making them likely to be nouns, maybe personal names
or place names. That they shared the same context was of course essential, otherwise she might have been comparing groups of three words that
were visually similar but, unknown to her, were grammatically *dis*similar,
which would have rendered a comparison invalid and potentially misleading. (A very rough equivalent might be a comparison of three bus
timetables for the same route, one for daytime, the second for night-time
and the third for Sundays. This would be valid because the context is the
same, whereas a comparison of daytime timetables for three related but
different routes would be potentially misleading, even though they might
easily share some bus-stop names in common.)

Here are two of Kober's 'triplets':

We can see the inflection more clearly if we highlight the word endings:

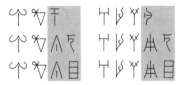

An English parallel might be:

Ca-na-da   Ar-ge(n)-ti-na
Ca-na-di-a(n)   Ar-ge(n)-ti-ni-a(n)
Ca-na-di-a(ns)   Ar-ge(n)-ti-ni-a(ns)

If such parallels were right (assuming that Linear B was syllabic, like the Cypriot script), 𐊗 and 𐊢 would have different consonants (C) but share the same vowel (V), like *da* and *na* in Cana-**da**/Argenti-**na**, i.e.:

So would 𐊍 and 𐊐 like *di* and *ni* in Cana-**di**-a(n)/Argenti-**ni**-a(n):

	V1	**V2**
C_1	𐊗	𐊍
C_2	𐊢	𐊐

By the same token, using the other three 'triplets', Kober arrived at what she called 'the beginning of a tentative phonetic pattern':

	V1	**V2**
C_1	𐊗	𐊍
C_2	𐊢	𐊐
C_3	𐊜s	𐊌
C_4	𐊕	𐊋
C_5	𐊏	𐊒

The phonetic values of these syllabic signs were as yet undetermined, but their interrelationships – on the model of the blank square in a crossword where two words meet in which the shared letter is unknown yet must fit the two words – were (tentatively) established. This analytical principle, called a 'grid' by Ventris and others, was seminal in organizing the bewildering mass of inscriptions for decipherment. The concept of a grid, though not the actual word, was not new – it was used in the 19th century in the cuneiform and other decipherments – but it came into its own with Linear B.

Original as the above insight was, Kober somewhat spoilt it by giving a strong hint in one of her papers that she thought the 'triplets' were cases of a noun on the Latin model (e.g. domin**us**/domin**i**/domin**o**). She was wrong about this, as we shall see. On the other hand, careful scholar that she was, in a later paper she did not repeat the Latin parallel but instead contented herself with the observation that, 'There is enough evidence to make it necessary to investigate the inflection theory thoroughly, and without prejudice. If it is right, more evidence will appear; if more evidence is not found, it is wrong.'

One other result by Kober must be mentioned, without going into her detailed reasons. She demonstrated that the two Linear B words for 'total' (page 25), ╤ ⸋ and ╤ Ⲩ, are masculine and feminine variants of the same root word: the first appears with the 'man' logogram and male animals, the second with the 'woman' logogram and female animals. Since both words contain two signs, of which the first is the same, the variant was clearly formed by a change of vowel (or conceivably consonant) rather than by the addition of an extra syllable. The importance of this deduction lies in the fact that Indo-European languages are almost alone in this formation. Hence the language of Linear B was very likely to be Indo-European (which included Greek), and not Semitic or similar to Etruscan, the candidate favoured by Ventris. As for the language of Linear A, Kober had no truck with the lazy consensus that it must be the same as that of Linear B because the two scripts looked quite similar and were found in similar contexts; she pointed out, perfectly logically, that modern roman scripts look similar but are used to write quite unrelated languages. Linear A, she thought, probably wrote a different language from Linear B.

During 1948, an already-ailing Kober virtually bowed out of the Linear B battle with these words, in her article 'The Minoan scripts: fact and theory': 'When we have the facts, certain conclusions will be almost inevitable. Until we have them, no conclusions are possible.' Ventris read the piece and criticized it to Myres for ending on 'a rather pessimistic note'. In correspondence with Kober, and when they met in Oxford in 1948, Ventris and she developed little rapport. Although he undoubtedly learnt from her work and would later praise some aspects, he never went back on his basic view that she was too negative about the prospects of a decipherment.

Surely, she did go too far in her article. No science, and certainly no archaeological decipherment, proceeds on such an arid, all-or-nothing basis. The scientist and the decipherer never have all the facts they need, but when they have sufficient to form sensible hypotheses, they can hope to test these hypotheses against existing knowledge and against new facts as these become available. This is where the element of creativity and courage comes in. Alice Kober was probably too restrained a scholar to have 'cracked' Linear B. In the published words of Ventris written after the decipherment, her approach was 'prim but necessary' (privately, he told another American woman scholar that Kober's logic was 'a shade too frigid and destructive for my taste!'). To go further would require a mind like his, that combined her perseverance, logic and method with a willingness to take intellectual risks.

To return to Ventris in August 1948, he did indeed 'stick to his own last' – at least for a while. Abandoning Myres's transcription project, in September he and Graeme Shankland started a year-long course in town planning, a relatively new subject which had acquired real importance with the crucial Town and Country Planning Act of 1947. But Ventris was distinctly dissatisfied with the course. The subject was rather nebulous and ill defined and the course was poorly presented, according to Shankland. 'Michael was deeply furious about the sloppy and illogical way that most of the lectures were put together.... He found it irritating to be taught by men who were ignorant of logic.'

However he stuck it out, was awarded a diploma, and in September 1949 joined the Ministry of Education as part of a development group of architects dedicated to the design of new schools, who were located in breeze-block offices with regulation 'battleship grey' linoleum floors in a central government building in Curzon Street (later well known to Londoners for being occupied by the secret service). This work was more satisfying than the planning course, because it had a definite focus for new thinking and design: the need to put into practical effect the large expansion of state education legislated by the Butler Act of 1944. School teaching was becoming less rigid and more liberal, and the era of open-plan classrooms, movable desks, learning by doing, bright colours and a generally less 'Victorian' educational environment, was dawning. A fellow architect and graduate of the AA, who joined the group at exactly the same time, Dargan Bullivant, remembers quite an intense, even intellectual atmosphere in the office, influenced by two slightly more senior figures, Mary Crowley and David Medd, a childless, husband-and-wife team reminiscent of the formidable Fabian team of Beatrice and Sidney Webb. Bullivant soon realized that Ventris was 'an intellectual aristocrat', though he found him to be easy company, never a show-off: 'he was not a natural expositor, and if you didn't follow him the first time, you would not feel you could ask him again. But he didn't try to humiliate you with his cleverness.'

From surviving drawings of a school by Ventris, he clearly worked to his usual clean-lined, fastidious standards. Still, it is hard to see how designing schools could have excited or challenged his mind for long – especially as he had an aversion for 'sharawaggi' in design, had not much enjoyed his own school days, and was not very interested in children. Soon, his mind was moving on. A younger architect in the office who became a friend, Edward Samuel, remembered that during lunch breaks Ventris would work on Linear A and Linear B (Samuel would help him look for similarities of sign in the text on different tablets), and he would make phone calls to his stockbroker; once, he told Samuel after finishing a call that he had just made more money in that one call than his entire year's salary. He was also deeply involved, outside the office, in assembling a 'Guide to Modern Architecture in Western Europe 1900–1950', naturally including all the buildings he admired in Copenhagen and in Sweden, which was based on a survey questionnaire of his own design circulated among architects in Britain and on the Continent. And he was looking for other architectural work: for example, a Festival of Britain Information Office in Leicester Square, which he and Oliver Cox designed together.

His small spring-backed, loose-leaf design book for this modest project still exists, dated October 1949. Interleaved among the sketches of the room, its furniture and various gadgets, are lists of Linear B sign groups with possible Etruscan parallels. There can be no more eloquent witness to the way in which design and decipherment ran along side by side in Ventris's complex mind.

A month or so later, while working at the Ministry of Education, he took his next major step towards the decipherment. His own introductory words describe it best. 'At the end of 1949 I sent out copies of the following questionnaire to a number of scholars who have been working in recent years on the problems set by the language and writing of the prehistoric Aegean, suggesting that we might make New Year 1950 the occasion for an informal exchange of views, reviewing the position reached at the end of the half-century' – i.e. 50 years after Evans first discovered the

Minoan scripts. 'The answers to the questionnaire are collected together in this progress report, which I have had duplicated and circulated privately at my own expense: a venture which enables me to add some notes of my own which are too disjointed for more formal publication.... I have, by general consent, typed the whole bulletin in English, translating a proportion of the contributions which were in French, German, Italian or Swedish; and must therefore take responsibility for any conclusions awkwardly or imperfectly expressed.'

The 'venture' – which Ventris also called 'an interesting experiment in international cooperation' and which soon became known as the *Mid-Century Report* – was wholly typical of him. No professional classicist would have conceived it, and if one had, he or she would almost certainly have lacked the linguistic skills to translate the replies, which came from all over Europe and from the United States. It was 'group working' applied to a completely different field, the decipherment of the Minoan scripts, in a disinterested effort to break the scholarly impasse.

The questions were numerous, penetrating and detailed. For example:

1   What kind of language is represented in the Linear B inscriptions, and to what other known languages is it related?

8   Do you feel that certain distinctions should be made between particular Linear B signs which have tended to be confused in the signaries so far published?

10 If the signs are syllabic, what kind of syllables do they represent?

12 Is the Cypriot syllabary directly descended from the Minoan scripts?

17 To what extent are prefixes, or compounds, or suffixes, the typical mechanism for forming Minoan names?

20 Which sign groups in Linear B (and in Linear A if you consider the language identical) appear to be VOCABULARY WORDS (nouns, adjectives, pronouns, numerals, prepositions, adverbs, conjunctions) rather than proper names?

Several scholars wrote highly detailed responses, as did Ventris himself, and every scholar actively working on the Minoan scripts replied, except for two. The first was the Prague scholar Bedřich Hrozný, whose recent published decipherments of Linear B, the Indus Valley script and several other undeciphered scripts had been roundly rejected by scholars, despite his respected work during the first world war in deciphering Hittite cuneiform. ('From this occupational disease of decoders we may all wish to be preserved', wrote Ventris, after Hrozný's death.) The second was Alice Kober. She wrote testily: 'I have no intention of answering the questionnaire. In my opinion it represents a step in the wrong direction and is a complete waste of time.' By then she had only three months to live.

There was little consensus, however. Perhaps the most striking fact is that not a single scholar, including of course Ventris, ventured to suggest that Linear B's language might be Greek. Some thought the language might be Indo-European, others non-Indo-European, while Bennett and Myres (and of course Kober) refrained from speculation.

Ventris concluded his twenty-page response by stating: 'I have good hopes that a sufficient number of people working on these lines will before long enable a satisfactory solution to be found. To them I offer my best wishes, being forced by pressure of other work to make this my last small contribution to the problem.' For the rest of 1950, he went back to full-time architecture.

But, as ever, Linear B would not leave him be. During that year, the pace of his correspondence with Bennett quickened. In July, they met for the first time, in London, when Bennett visited Myres on his way to Greece. He showed Ventris some of the Pylos material, and they formed the beginnings of a friendship. In November, after reading an excellent article by Bennett (the one on the numerical systems of Linear A and B) in the *American Journal of Archaeology*, Ventris wrote that he was so excited he had to jump out of bed at 3 a.m. in order to jot down his (lengthy) response. Publication of the Pylos tablets was now scheduled for the spring of 1951, and surely the long-awaited Knossos tablets could not be much further off. The prospects for success were brightening. Soon, Ventris decided he must quit his job, draw upon his private income, and sit at home in Highpoint to concentrate exclusively on deciphering Linear B. Characteristically, he did not explain his reasons to any of his colleagues at the Ministry of Education.

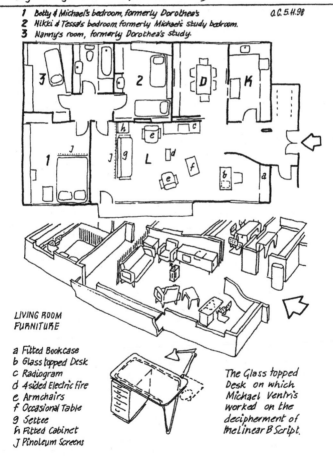

FLAT 47 HIGHPOINT : AS FURNISHED, 1950

Design & Layout of Loose & fitted furniture by FRS Yorke & Marcel Breuer '36

O.C. 5.11.98

1 Betty & Michael's bedroom, formerly Dorothea's
2 Nikki & Tessa's bedroom formerly Michael's study bedroom.
3 Nanny's room, formerly Dorothea's study.

LIVING ROOM
FURNITURE

a Fitted Bookcase
b Glass topped Desk
c Radiogram
d 4 sided Electric fire
e Armchairs
f Occasional Table
g Settee
h Fitted Cabinet
J Pinoleum Screens

The Glass topped Desk on which Michael Ventris worked on the decipherment of the Linear B Script.

A sketch of 47 Highpoint by Oliver Cox.

He would never really return to architecture. So maybe this is the moment, at the parting of his parallel careers, to summarize exactly what the two had in common. First of all, there is the problem-solving nature of architecture and decipherment: both architects and decipherers, at the most fundamental level, are looking for solutions to problems that satisfy a given set of constraints – whether these be that a design must fit a certain space or that a language must be Indo-European. Then there is the functional nature of both buildings and writing systems: both are designed by human beings to be used; neither is art for art's sake. As for the methods adopted by Ventris to solve design and decipherment problems, there can be no doubt that he applied group working to both architecture and Linear B; and that the way he would record all his 'working' on Linear B (including errors), in a series of twenty Work Notes, was a direct evolution of the detailed design books he kept as an architect. Finally, uniting fundamental similarities with methods, there is the way in which both architecture and decipherment require the mental manipulation of large amounts of visual and written data. Perhaps Chadwick – in one of his rare references to Ventris's work as an architect – put the link between one career and the other best when he wrote: 'The architect's eye sees in a building not a mere façade, a jumble of ornamental and structural features; it looks beneath the appearance and distinguishes the significant parts of the pattern, the structural elements and framework of the building. So too Ventris was able to discern among the bewildering variety of the mysterious signs, patterns and regularities which betrayed the underlying structure. It is this quality, the power of seeing order in apparent confusion, that has marked the work of all great men.'

Into the Minoan Labyrinth

'To wait for a bilingual to help us solve our problem
is to cry for the moon.'
Michael Ventris, Work Note 15, September 1951

A nd so, at the beginning of 1951, we reach the most intense
phase of Ventris's work on Linear B, which would culminate
a year and half later in his announcement of the decipherment. Writing after the event, in 1953, he set down the basics of his
approach in words so concise and masterly they are worth quoting,
before we try to understand the details of how he did it.

Any decipherment, he wrote, 'needs to be planned in three phases: an
exhaustive *analysis* of the signs, words and contexts in all the available
inscriptions, designed to extract every possible clue as to the spelling
system, meaning and language structure; an experimental *substitution* of
phonetic values to give possible words and inflections in a known or
postulated language; and a decisive *check*, preferably with the aid of
virgin material, to ensure that the apparent results are not due to fantasy,
coincidence or circular reasoning.... Prerequisites are that the material
should be large enough for the analysis to yield usable results, and (in the
case of an unreadable script without bilinguals or identifiable proper
names) that the concealed language should be related to one which we
already know.' With Linear B, the analysis phase lasted up to June 1952,

when the substitution phase took over and revealed that the language was probably Greek, which was then confirmed in the check phase after May 1953, when sensational virgin material from mainland Greece became available.

What makes Ventris's decipherment so remarkable is, of course, that before it took place the script was completely unreadable; there were few reliable clues to the concealed language (Ventris's guess, an Etruscan-related language, was entirely wrong); there were no bilinguals or identifiable proper names (no Rosetta stone or inscribed obelisks, containing predictable names like Ptolemy, Cleopatra and Alexander); and finally that, until 1952 when the Knossos tablets were published, Ventris had access to a rather limited quantity of material (unlike in the decipherment of Egyptian hieroglyphs, Babylonian cuneiform and Mayan glyphs).

'The main thing', Ventris told Bennett in mid-1951, 'is to discuss the data objectively, at this first stage, without looking forward to conclusions which one has reached by more experimental means.... You're less likely to put your foot wrong here than I am.' The nearly two hundred pages of his twenty Work Notes bear out his self-criticism. Densely typed (by Ventris himself, like all his work) and profusely illustrated with his own Linear B signs, they overflow with highly ingenious linguistic analysis, hypothesis and experiment, jumping back and forth between these modes of attack and between a bewildering range of Linear B inscriptions (buttressed with references to inscriptions from other languages and neighbouring civilizations). And naturally the notes show only what Ventris chose to commit to paper, not the mental gymnastics and intuitive leaps that led to the words on the page; these can only be conjectured. 'If the secret of the Linear B labyrinth was at some points penetrable, he was the man to penetrate it, thanks to his scouting and his probing', a scholar wrote much later. But there is unfortunately no thread like Ariadne's running through the labyrinth. John Chadwick admitted as much, and in *The Decipherment of Linear B* made little attempt to present the decipherment in the same order as the Work Notes. Even Ventris, despite his best efforts, was unable to produce a coherent narrative of his method (like Champollion, it is interesting to note); and he went so far as to advise Chadwick that Work Note 19 – written a mere two months before his breakthrough – was in fact 'complete nonsense'. So we must, I fear, be humbly content with a summary of Ventris's key techniques and conclusions, based on his own simplified account supplemented by his Work Notes and letters to Myres and Bennett, followed by a fuller explanation of what was unquestionably his moment of revelation.

To kick off, let us look at the 'grid', mentioned in the last chapter in connection with Alice Kober's analyses of the unknown vowels and consonants in the syllables of Linear B. Not only do Ventris grids exist in paper form in three of the Work Notes, Ventris also constructed a physical grid which he could play with whenever he felt like trying out a new move. An architect friend, Michael Grice, who used to visit 47 Highpoint, remembered seeing an array of labels with Linear B signs written on them hanging from hooks in a wooden board fixed to a wall of the flat. Although Ventris characteristically did not talk about his toy, Grice was struck by how similar it was in concept to the way in which architects think about solving problems. (Sadly, unlike Crick and Watson's almost equally primitive metal 'double helix' model of DNA, now in the Science Museum in London, Ventris's model is not to be found in any 'museum of decipherment', because it no longer exists.)

The very first Work Note, dated 28 January 1951, contains a grid, with vowels down the columns and consonants across the rows. Ventris has experimentally placed a range of signs on it, according to the interrelationships he had worked out from the few published tablets; some of these signs would turn out to be in the correct position. He has also guessed some phonetic values on the basis of Etruscan analogies; these values were mostly incorrect, as might be expected.

'B' SYLLABARY PHONETIC 'GRID'

Fig. 1
MGFV

1: State as at 28 Jan 51 : before publication of Pylos inscriptions.

CONSONANTS	Vowel 1 NIL? (-o?) = typical 'nominative' of nouns which change their last theme syllable in oblique cases	Vowel 2 -i? = typical changed last syllable before -ζ and -Β.	Other vowels? -a,-e,-u? = changes in last syllable caused by other endings. (5 vowels in all, rather than 4?)	Doubtful
1 t- ?	Ŧ ag	⋔ aj		⊕ ax (Sundwall)
2 r- ??	ꙅ az	Ħ iw	⋔ ah ⋀ ol	
3 ś- ??	Ψ eg	Ħ aw	⋣ oc Ʌ oj	
4 n- ?? s- ??	⧖ od	⋔ ok	⋔ ib	T̄ is ⋔ oh
5		A ak	Ψ ef	
6 l- ?	† ac	ⅼ⊆ ij		
7 h- ??	⊘ ix		⋙ if	
8 θ- ??	⋓ en		⋙ id	⋔ ex
9 m- ? k- ?	⊙ ay	–if an enclitic "and".		⋔ al
10				⌇ om ☰ av
11				
12				
13				
14				
15				

⋔ aj   ⅼ⊆ ij   A ak   ⋔ il   Ħ aw   ⋔ og   Ψ ej   ⋔ oh   ⅼꙅ er   Ʌ oj   ⋔ ex   ⋔ ok   ⋔ ib   Ħ iw

← group of syllables, including those occurring before -Β on 'woman' tablet (Hr 44, PM fig 689), and those characteristic of alternating endings -ζ & -Β. About ¾ of these 14 signs very likely include vowel 2.

Ventris's phonetic 'grid' from Work Note 1, January 1951.
(Ignore the labels such as 'ag', 'id' and 'ol' which are not proposed phonetic values.)

As the Work Notes progressed, the grid steadily filled up with Linear B signs like words in a crossword, while Ventris dropped or refined his guesses at the phonetic values of the vowels and consonants. Although the positions of the signs continued to be revised, the grid endured – and assisted Ventris to predict, if only very tentatively, new interrelationships between signs, as when a crossword is gradually completed. According to Ventris and Chadwick, writing after the breakthrough: 'The problem of decipherment is in this way reduced to the correct distribution of five vowels and twelve consonants to the columns of the grid; and since a proposed reading of only two or three words may, by a "chain-reaction", predetermine rigid values for almost the entire syllabary, a very severe discipline is imposed on the earliest stages of a decipherment. If the initial moves are wrong, it should be quite impossible to force any part of the texts into showing the slightest conformity with the vocabulary or grammar of a known language; even though that might be quite easy if one were free to juggle with the values of 88 mutually unconnected signs.' While this was true in principle, in practice the Linear B grid never played as decisive a role in the decipherment as their statement implies.

The first substantial progress was possible when Ventris received *The Pylos Tablets: A Preliminary Transcription* from Bennett in March 1951. At this time, even six years after the end of the war, Britain still had rationing and a relatively austere regime; gifts from the United States were especially welcome, though carefully vetted by customs. An amused Bennett recalled decades later that he received a letter of thanks from Ventris explaining how when he went to pick up the packet containing Bennett's small book, a suspicious London postal official asked him: 'I see the contents are listed as PYLOS TABLETS. Now, just what ailments are pylos tablets supposed to alleviate?'

In Work Note 7, dated 1 May, his first note on the Pylos tablets, Ventris recorded a series of important 'assumptions and objectives' behind his approach:

1 Until the Pylos material has been fully analysed, or until the Knossos material is published, discussion is best confined to the Pylos tablets, and the Knossos evidence only brought in where a definite analogy is helpful on a specific problem.

2 Conclusions drawn from an initial analysis of the Pylos inscriptions must be regarded as tentative until the whole of the Knossos material has been published, and, in the case of fragmentary evidence, until the transcriptions have been collated with the originals.

3 In spite of slight differences in script and in accounting method which suggest a different date and place of origin, the Knossos and Pylos tablets are written in the same language, which is not Greek....

4 The theory that Minoan Linear B is an early dialect of the Etruscan-Lemnian family is to be constantly tested against apparent meanings and inflections – but not to the exclusion of possible analogies with other language groups.

5 Each of the 79 'syllabic' signs...is purely phonetic in *every* sign group in Bennett's index, even if some sign groups are occasionally abbreviated.... This means that the initial analysis can take no account of the *shapes* of signs used in sign groups. [Ventris mentions 79, not 89, signs, because he has excluded ten signs as being too rare for useful analysis.]

6 Identifications of Minoan signs with Cypriot syllables must be confirmed by linguistic evidence, and not based upon superficial resemblances, however methodically these are applied....

7 The simplest, most mundane and least surprising explanation of any inscription is likely to be the correct one. Both the archive tablets and the Minoan inscriptions written on other objects are likely to have the same general content as similarly written inscriptions from cultures near in time and space...[e.g. Mesopotamia].

8 We may never succeed in fully interpreting these tablets, since we should probably not be able to understand more than a small part of

the Minoan vocabulary even if we knew how it was pronounced. Our limited objective must be to give phonetic values to the majority of the signs, and thereby to define at least the general nature of the Minoan language....

Unsurprisingly, the assumption that the Linear B language was 'not Greek' got a rise out of the ever-cautious Bennett. In reply, Ventris asked him jokingly whether he was 'secretly cooking up a Greek decipherment – out with it!'

His first technique was statistical, of the kind introduced earlier when discussing Bennett's signary of Linear B. Using Bennett's transcription of the tablets from Pylos, Ventris counted each sign group (word) with a distinct spelling, and discarded recurring sign groups. (This was necessary to avoid distortion of the statistics by counting multiple occurrences of common words, including names.) It left him with 5410 total occurrences of signs. He then counted the number of occurrences of each of 79 signs, taken from Bennett's 89-sign list, and calculated their frequencies out of 1000. This enabled him to classify the 79 signs into three categories: Frequent (15 signs), Average (26 signs) and Infrequent (38 signs). In addition, he classified each sign according to its *position* in sign groups, such as initial, final, second or all positions. Overleaf is the sign frequency table he produced in Work Note 8. Note that the three signs Ⱶ, Ⱳ, and Ⱪ – which include the 'double-axe' and the 'throne-and-sceptre' – have high frequencies in the initial position. This suggested to Ventris that they were probably *pure vowels*. The reason is that in a syllabary of the CV ('open') type, the sign for a pure vowel will occur mainly at the beginning of a word, because in every other position a vowel will normally be subsumed into the syllabic sign. Thus, in English, 'operator' would be spelt syllabically *o-pe-ra-to-r(o)* and 'anagram' *a-na-g(a)-ra-m(a)*, with no pure vowels except in initial position. A pure vowel would appear *within* a word only in examples such as 'initial', *i-ni-ti-a-l(a)* or 'anionic', *a-ni-o-ni-c(i)*.

FIGURE 7: Minoan B syllabary.

Ventris
WORK NOTE
1 May 51

PYLOS SIGNS IN ORDER OF FREQUENCY

FREQUENT SIGNS

1 : om 44.0	FINAL , rare initial & second	6 : an 34.0	final and penultimate	11 : ij 31.2	SECOND
2 : af 38.2	penultimate	7 : ac 33.8	final & second, rare initial	12 : ik 30.3	INITIAL & final, rare second
3 : ak 37.7	INITIAL	8 : ix 33.1	all positions	13 : av 29.4	FINAL rare initial
4 : ig 37.2	INITIAL rare elsewhere	9 : iw 32.5	final	14 : ag 28.6	final & second
5 : eg 34.4	second and penultimate	10 : if 32.3	second and initial	15 : oj 28.1	final and penultimate

AVERAGE SIGNS

16 : ax 24.0	initial and second	25 : aj 17.0	penultimate and second	34 : id 12.9	FINAL
17 : og 22.2	SECOND & penult, rare Final	26 : ef 17.0	initial and penultimate	35 : il 12.6	SECOND rare Final
18 : az 21.2	FINAL	27 : on 15.2	penultimate and second	36 : od 10.3	infreq initial, otherwise all
19 : en 20.5	FINAL rare initial	28 : ej 14.8	final	37 : ez 10.2	infrequent Final, otherwise all
20 : al 19.6	second	29 : ol 14.8	penultimate and second, rare Final	38 : ab 10.0	infrequent Final, otherwise all
21 : aw 18.8	all positions	30 : is 14.4	rare initial, otherwise all	39 : iu 9.4	all positions
22 : ok 17.7	penultimate and Final	31 : ay 14.2	FINAL see Note 10 !	40 : eu 9.2	infrequent Final, otherwise all
23 : ap 17.5	INITIAL	32 : ad 13.7	INITIAL infrequent final	41 : eh 8.3	SECOND rare final
24 : oh 17.2	penultimate and initial	33 : ih 13.5	INITIAL infrequent final		

INFREQUENT SIGNS

42 : ib 7.4	PENULTIMATE, not initial	55 : ip 3.3	INITIAL not final	68 : ett 0.7	not initial
43 : ew 6.8	rare final, otherwise all	56 : oz 2.8	practically only INITIAL	69 : os 0.7	initial only
44 : es 6.3	INITIAL infrequent final	57 : ed 2.4	rare final, otherwise all	70 : ecc 0.6	initial only
45 : er 6.1	rare final	58 : im 2.4	penultimate and initial	71 : ov 0.6	not initial
46 : oc 6.1	FINAL	59 : iq 2.4	SECOND	72 : ar 0.4	not initial
47 : ek 5.7	initial	60 : ih 2.2	rare initial, otherwise all	73 : eo 0.4	not initial
48 : ep 5.4	PENULTIMATE, infreq initial	61 : oi 1.5	SECOND, not initial or final	74 : eq 0.4	final only
49 : el 5.0	all positions	62 : ei 1.3	FINAL not initial	75 : iz 0.4	final only
50 : iv 5.0	INITIAL not final	63 : ess 1.3	PENULTIMATE	76 : ob 0.4	second only
51 : at 4.1	rare final, not initial	64 : ox 1.3	INITIAL not final	77 : or 0.4	second only
52 : ex 4.1	PENULTIMATE, not initial or final	65 : am 1.1	not penultimate or final	78 : oe 0.2	second only
53 : in 4.1	INITIAL not final	66 : ec 0.9	INITIAL not final	79 : op 0.2	second only
54 : eb 3.5	not initial, otherwise all	67 : of 0.9	SECOND		

Overall frequencies PER THOUSAND calculated on 5,410 total occurrences recorded

Sign frequency table from Work Note 8, May 1951.

The latter type of word turns out to be comparatively infrequent, whatever the language under consideration. (Fifteen minutes spent scanning an English dictionary will prove the point.)

Other useful frequency analysis concerned sign combinations, e.g. two signs adjacent to one another in a sign group, since each language is characterized by certain frequent combinations of signs (such as 'th', 'io' or 'qu' in English) and infrequent combinations (such as 'dh', 'ao' or 'qi'). But as Ventris admitted, frequency analysis has major limitations as a decipherment tool. He told Myres: 'You are...quite right to be sceptical of the value of statistical studies as a *direct* key to decipherment: but I feel they are necessary to sketch in the background of fact against which any proposed decipherment will have to be tested.'

Another sign ☺ ('button') was found to occur with 'average' frequency but apparently exclusively in the final position of sign groups, as in the following tablet:

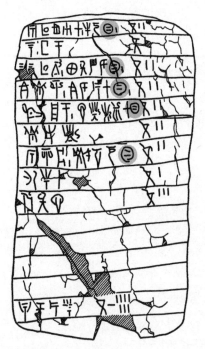

That the 'button' sign was a suffix and not part of the root was clear from the fact that there occurred pairs of sign groups of the following kind:

W-X-Y-Z

W-X-Y-Z-☺

This suggested to Ventris that the 'button' might be a conjunction such as 'and', formed not in the English way as a separate word but as a syllable tacked on to the preceding word, like '-te' in ancient Greek and '-que' in the Latin phrase 'Senatus Populus*que* Romanus' (SPQR), meaning 'The Senate *and* People of Rome'. In English, '-ly' is tacked on to adjectives to form adverbs in the same way (e.g. quick-ly).

However, in a lengthy discussion of ☺ in Work Note 10, Ventris was cautious of jumping to the conclusions that, first, *all* occurrences of the 'button' sign meant 'and' and, second, the sign was the *only* way to write 'and' in Linear B. For he had noted certain final-position occurrences in sign groups where the 'button' sign did not appear to mean 'and' from its context (indeed the sign would later turn up functioning as an ordinary syllabic sign at the *beginning* of some Pylos sign groups). Also, he knew that Latin, for example, has the very common discrete conjunction 'et' meaning 'and', as well as the tacked-on '-que'. Lastly, he had noticed sign groups in the Pylos tablets which were apparently linked in sense by 'and' but where there was no 'button' sign written (as in English we write a list such as 'London, Paris, Amsterdam and Berlin' without writing 'and' between the first three cities).

Then there was the technique of scribal variation – the subject of Work Note 9 (written, somewhat confusingly, after Work Note 10 on 'Minoan' conjunctions). In other words, a search for variant spellings of the same word, such as 'recogni**s**e/recogni**z**e', 'encyclop**ae**dia/encyclo-p**e**dia' in English. Ventris looked for pairs of Linear B sign groups which appeared in two slightly different spellings, for example:

1	2	3
�879/�879	⊻ΧΥ𐅆/⊻ΑΥ𐅆	⊻‡Χ⊼Λ/Α‡Χ⊼Λ

and he deduced that there was a close relationship between a sign in one group and the sign that had replaced it in the second group (perhaps a shared vowel but different consonant). For this technique to work, the two words have to be semantically the same and differ only graphically (by one or perhaps two signs), e.g. cent**er**/cent**re**, s**c**eptical/s**k**eptical, infle**ct**ion/infle**x**ion, trave**l**er/trave**ll**er, jewe**l**ry/jewe**ll**ery, and must not be two words of completely different meaning, such as but**t**er/but**l**er, **y**ellow/**b**ellow, fri**ct**ion/fra**ct**ion, **pre**scribe/**pro**scribe, which happen to have one sign different but are unrelated in their meaning. The obvious problem is how to establish this when one cannot read the language. The most promising examples in Linear B came from pairs of long words, or from scribal erasures of spelling mistakes in which it sometimes proved possible to read both the intended sign and the old, erased sign beneath it.

The existence of such 3500-year-old clay-tablet 'rubbings out' alerted Ventris to the possibility of *uncorrected* spelling mistakes in the tablets – which most certainly occur in cuneiform tablets and in Egyptian hieroglyphic inscriptions. 'Since we are still so far from a full understanding of the Pylos inscriptions, it is perhaps rather presumptuous to point to any spellings in the sign group index as actual *mistakes* on the part of the Minoan scribe. Nevertheless there are a number of spellings which must look anomalous even to us', Ventris noted. And he turned out to be right in this assumption: some Minoan scribes were more careful writers, or at least better spellers, than others.

But the most far-reaching technique used by Ventris – which he applied in the later Work Notes from the early summer of 1951 onwards, first to the Pylos tablets and then from April 1952 to the Knossos tablets (published in *Scripta Minoa*, volume 2) – was to search the sign groups for patterns of inflection. Evans had doodled this idea in the 1930s; Kober had drawn the inflectional ground plan in the 1940s; Ventris would design the elevations and build the structure in the 1950s.

In mid-June 1951, on this topic he wrote: 'It is possible to disagree here and there on whether a particular pair of sign groups really are inflected forms of the same word; but the basic existence of inflection, hinted at by Evans and confirmed with rather ponderous logic by Kober, is now beyond doubt. I must admit though, that at the time of Kober's articles [i.e. up to 1948] on the subject I was inclined to follow Myres in dismissing most of her evidence for inflection as being merely alternative name endings' – something like, to take a not-so-satisfactory English parallel, Parkins/Parkinson, Robins/Robinson, in which the name change could give the misleading appearance of being an inflection formed by adding '-on' to the root. (This distinction – between inflection and alternative name endings – would prove highly relevant at the time of breakthrough in the decipherment.) By late August, he was willing to be more definite still: 'the large and very interesting body of evidence which can be extracted from [the Pylos sign groups] makes the presence of inflection, first seriously demonstrated by Kober, a certainty.' In due course, Ventris would be prepared to give the late American scholar further credit for her work on inflection, but he would never be warm in his praise. And given the consistent cold shoulder he had received from her throughout, even before her illness, one does not feel inclined to criticize him. (Champollion was far *less* generous to Young in the Egyptian decipherment.)

In Work Note 11, Ventris studied the question of inflection for *gender*. This is characteristic of common nouns in some Indo-European languages such as ancient Greek (e.g. doul**os**/doul**ē**, 'slave'), Latin (domi-n**us**/domin**a,** 'master/mistress') and Italian (bambin**o**/bambin**a**, 'child'), but not Danish or English; although English does use a few forms like 'prince/princess', the vast majority of common nouns do not vary with gender. Such gender distinction is also found in some non-Indo-European languages, though not in Etruscan, so far as we know from our very limited grasp of the language (Etruscan proper names take a feminine form, but common nouns do not).

From the evidence of the Linear B tablets, it looked to Ventris as if the language did mark masculine and feminine forms – as seen in the following pairs of sign groups, in which the discrimination between the masculine and feminine forms is based on the adjacency of these sign groups to masculine and feminine pictograms/logograms (see page 25):

masculine

𐀷𐀙 𐀴𐀯 𐀹𐀀𐀵 𐀵𐀺𐀼𐀐𐀁 𐀺𐀫𐀆 𐀵𐀬𐀵𐀁𐀍𐀡𐀈

feminine

𐀷𐀫 𐀴𐀺 𐀹𐀀𐀬 𐀵𐀺𐀼𐀐𐀊 𐀺𐀫𐀄 𐀵𐀬𐀵𐀁𐀍𐀡𐀍

These comparisons were of course grist to the grid, since they suggested that the final sign in each pair of sign groups shared either the same consonant (or conceivably the same vowel). From their contexts on the tablets, the first three pairs appeared to mean: 'child' (boy/girl); 'total' (male/female) – this guess had already been made by Evans and settled by Kober, as we know; and thirdly, 'slave' (male/female).

Inflection based on *number*, in other words singular and plural forms, was useful too. Where there were numerals on the tablets, singular and plural forms could often be distinguished; a numeral 1 obviously implied a singular form for the adjacent sign group. In English, noun plurals are generally inflected with the addition of an '-s' or '-es', or perhaps a change of syllable (e.g. woman/women) or even the addition of a syllable (child/children) – but there are some nouns that do not change (e.g. sheep, species). In Linear B, some sign groups seemed to be the same in both the singular and the plural, i.e. they did not inflect, while others showed the addition of an extra syllable (highlighted):

singular

𐀷𐀙 𐀷𐀫 𐀹𐀀𐀵 𐀹𐀀𐀬 | 𐀀𐀁 𐀵𐀁𐀈 𐀬𐀪 𐀹𐀺𐀈

plural

𐀷𐀙 𐀷𐀫 𐀹𐀀𐀵 𐀹𐀀𐀬 | 𐀀𐀁𐀀 𐀵𐀁𐀈𐀀 𐀬𐀪𐀺 𐀹𐀺𐀈𐀺

(The first four pairs were encountered above in relation to gender inflection.) Ventris observed that the plural inflection in the second group resembled the formation of plurals in Greek, but the lack of change shown by the first four plurals was surprising.

Thirdly, Ventris searched for patterns of inflection by *case* in what appeared to be nouns, following on directly from Kober and her 'triplets'. But while Kober's 'triplets' had been taken from the few tablets that had been published in 1946 (those from Knossos), Ventris was able to retrieve many more of such patterns from an exhaustive search of the Pylos sign groups, always bearing in mind, as Kober and Bennett had, that the *context* of the sign groups he was comparing must be similar. According to him, certain sign groups that he judged from their context to spell men's names inflected in three 'cases' – nominative, genitive and dative (here called 'prepositional' because of some uncertainty) – but they followed at least six different types of declension. (Six may seem unduly complicated, but there are three noun declensions in ancient Greek and five in Latin.) Among the examples of this he reported in Work Note 14, in late August 1951, were the following:

Nominative

〔Linear B sign groups〕

Genitive

〔Linear B sign groups〕

'Prepositional'

〔Linear B sign groups〕

Again, it was possible to guess that the syllabic signs representing the case suffixes, added to the root in each declension, would be likely to share a vowel or consonant; but caution was required, given the complexity of the declensions.

At this point, with Work Note 15, Ventris produced a second grid. Compiled in Athens and dated 28 September 1951 (he was then on his

LINEAR SCRIPT B SYLLABIC GRID
(2ND STATE)

WORK NOTE 15
FIGURE 10
ATHENS, 28 SEPT 51

DIAGNOSIS OF CONSONANT AND VOWEL EQUATIONS
IN THE INFLEXIONAL MATERIAL FROM PYLOS:

THESE 51 SIGNS MAKE UP 90% OF ALL SIGN-OCCURRENCES IN THE PYLOS SIGNGROUP INDEX. APPENDED FIGURES GIVE EACH SIGN'S OVERALL FREQUENCY PER MILLE IN THE PYLOS INDEX.	"Impure" ending, typical syllables before -ᠯ & -ᛝ in Case 2c & 3	"Pure" ending, typical nominatives of forms in Column I	Includes possible "accusatives"	Also, but less frequently, the nominatives of forms in Column I	
	THESE SIGNS DON'T OCCUR BEFORE -ᛝ-	THESE SIGNS OCCUR LESS COMMONLY OR NOT AT ALL BEFORE -ᛝ-			
	MORE OFTEN FEMININE THAN MASCULINE?	MORE OFTEN MASCULINE THAN FEMININE?			MORE OFTEN FEMININE THAN MASCULINE?
	NORMALLY FORM THE GENITIVE SINGULAR BY ADDING -ᠯ	NORMALLY FORM THE GENITIVE SINGULAR BY ADDING -ᛝ			
	vowel 1	vowel 2	vowel 3	vowel 4	vowel 5
pure vowels?	30.3				37.2
a semi-vowel?				34.0	29.4
consonant 1	14.8	32.5	21.2	28.1	18.8
2	19.6	17.5			13.7
3		9.2		3.3	10.0
4	17.0	28.6			0.4
5	17.7	10.3		4.1	10.2
6	7.4	20.5		14.8	14.4
7	4.1	44.0			
8	6.1	6.1		13.5	15.2
9		33.1		32.3	2.4
10	22.2		38.2	3.5	2.2
11	31.2	33.8	34.4	8.3	0.7
12	17.0			37.7	24.0
13		9.4	14.2		
14	5.0				
15	12.6				

MICHAEL VENTRIS

Ventris's second syllabic grid, from Work Note 15, September 1951.

first visit to Greece, including Knossos), it is a big improvement on the first grid. Not only are more signs placed on it, they are more accurately positioned (judging of course with post-decipherment hindsight). But what is perhaps most striking is Ventris's cautious avoidance of phonetic values, as compared to the first grid. He shows none. Clearly, his intensive study of the Pylos tablets – indicated by his notes at the head of the columns of the grid – had convinced him that he should try to avoid some of his earlier shaky procedures, such as allotting possible phonetic values on the basis of Etruscan analogies.

He commented: 'the evidence which [the grid] offers now for phonetic values is not complete in itself,' i.e. it was too soon for the substitution phase of the decipherment mentioned earlier. Then he outlined his view of future work: more analysis of the case endings of proper names; comparison of sign frequencies and sign combination frequencies with syllabic frequencies in known languages; study of the connections between the Cypriot syllabary and Linear A/B; comparison of Linear A with Linear B; and most important of all, study of the Knossos tablets, as yet unpublished by Myres. But he admitted that it was 'doubtful' that phonetic values could be derived from these methods; at some point, it would be necessary to substitute at least some phonetic values derived from a known language chosen because it resembled the 'inflectional endings, vocabulary words and proper names' of 'Minoan'. For as he said, 'to wait for a *bilingual* to help us to solve our problem is to cry for the moon.' There was no Linear B equivalent of the Rosetta stone, and no practical prospect of finding one.

Deeply fascinated as he was by the problem, even Ventris was feeling the strain – not least because he had found and purchased a plot of land in Hampstead where he wanted to build the family house he and his wife had been discussing for almost ten years. He told Bennett in early September: 'this summer's work has rather upset my home life, and I'd like to ration my Minoan...during the next twelve-month.' In Work Note 15, he chided everyone on the circulation list (now 31 scholars): 'At the time of our joint Bulletin of 1950 [the *Mid-Century Report*], I had in mind to give up active Minoan studies owing to pressure of other work. I am now afraid that the considerable volume of these "Work Notes" may seem ironically to give the lie to this protestation, and that I may seem to have bitten off a more greedy chunk of the research than I can chew.... However, the other work still presses, and I should be very glad to see these studies taken further by others with whose methods I [am] in sympathy. I must put it on record, though, that at this writing only our colleagues in the United States [the now-dead Kober, and Bennett] seem to me to have so far shown the realistic approach. It is up to us in Europe to redress the balance.'

Strange though it may seem, at no time in his life would Ventris regard the decipherment of Linear B as a competitive race. Acting in the spirit of 'group working', his Work Notes and personal letters to scholars prove that he was always genuinely pleased to see others make progress in the field. Sometimes, one even has the sense that he would prefer *not* to be the one who would finally 'crack' the code. All the time he was obsessed with the subject, some part of him seems to have felt that he should be pursuing something else: the neglected architectural work for which he had been trained.

Nevertheless, there were two more mailings of extensive Work Notes before the end of 1951. Then Ventris and his wife left London for a three-week skiing holiday in Europe. But by the end of January 1952, he was back again in the Highpoint flat, hard at work reviewing the Pylos tablets and preparing for the arrival within a couple of months of *Scripta Minoa*, volume 2.

Work Note 17, dated 15 February 1952, contains a third, and final, grid. This time, phonetic values, for both vowels and consonants, have reappeared. How did Ventris arrive at them? According to him, 'The tentative phonetic values shown in the first column [i.e. the consonants] are

Ventris's third and final grid, from Work Note 17, February 1952.

not to be taken too seriously. They pay scarcely any regard to supposed similarities with the Cypriot syllabary, but represent the values which seem the most useful in giving an "Etruscoid" character to the Pylos names, words and inflections. This is still at the moment a very experimental procedure, but I am optimistic that before long it will prove the key to a reliable transliteration of the syllabary.'

In fact, his first guesses for the vocalic values in the vowel columns, *i*, *o*, *e* and *a* – are predominantly correct, being based partly on pure vowels' high frequency of occurrence as initial signs; while his guesses for the consonants are mainly wrong, deriving as they do from his tenaciously held, but incorrect, theory that 'Minoan' was related to Etruscan. Furthermore, the few syllabic signs which are correct, such as C_3V_5 (‡) = *pa* and C_6V_2 (Ŧ) = *to*, may have been influenced, consciously or unconsciously, by the resemblance of these two signs to the Cypriot signs for *pa* and *to*, despite Ventris's disclaimer. (See the Cypriot syllabary on page 35.) All in all, the grid was a mixture of logic and intuition: a useful experimental tool, but far from infallible. It was emphatically *not* the unique technique that would unlock Linear B.

A mere week after producing the third grid, Ventris's imagination was clearly in overdrive. The second volume of *Scripta Minoa* was yet to arrive, but still he wrote briefly to Myres about a particularly intriguing experiment he had tried over the weekend. For some time he had suspected that the Knossos tablets studied by Kober in the mid-1940s contained place names, and he knew that Myres agreed with him. In addition, he had noticed that Kober's particular 'triplets' occurred *only* in the tablets from Knossos, never in the tablets from Pylos. Could each 'triplet' refer to a different town in Crete? Now he noticed that if he made 'only a little adjustment' to the phonetic values that he had guessed in the grid, and then substituted them for the corresponding signs in Kober's 'triplets', a very interesting result emerged: what appeared to be archaic Greek names of three well-known Cretan cities, including Amnisos (the port of Knossos) and Knossos itself! 'This is one of those guesses it's best to keep up one's sleeve, because there's an extremely good chance of its being completely *wrong*', he told Myres cautiously. If correct, it suggested (but did not prove, since the words were place names and not common nouns), that the language of Linear B might be Greek. Ventris must have felt like Evans with the foal tablet (page 36): each man looked the 'Greek solution' in the face for a moment but pulled back on the brink of accepting it because he preferred another solution – 'Minoan' for Evans, 'Etruscan' for Ventris.

Yet he could not ignore his hunch. At the end of April, after receiving and immersing himself in Myres's massive edition of Evans's tablets from Knossos (and also dashing off some immaculate architectural plans for his new house), Ventris told Bennett: 'It would be a wonderful thing if one could sit down on the hill at Knossos and know just what the names of all the surrounding towns and villages were in Late Minoan times; because I'm sure some of them must occur [in these tablets]. I'm still rather intrigued by AMNISOS for 𐀀𐀖𐀛𐀰 [one of Kober's "triplets"].' As May wore on, he could not resist making further experiments with some phonetic values using his grid.

He began by allotting *a* to the 'double-axe' 𐀀, pure vowel 5 on the grid. Its already-mentioned high initial frequency in Linear B and similar behaviour in other languages suggested this identification to Ventris (and before him, Kober and a Greek scholar, K. D. Ktistopoulos). For his second guess he turned to the Cypriot clue once tried by Evans: comparison of the shapes of Linear B signs with those of the Cypriot script. Ventris had studiously avoided using this comparison until now – at least until the making of his third grid in early 1952 – because (like Evans) he distrusted it; but he had continued to believe in some kind of historic link between the languages of Crete, Cyprus and the Aegean area. He now hazarded that Linear B 𐀙 was equivalent to 𐠙 *-na* in Cypriot, and that Linear B 𐀴 was equivalent to 𐠯 *-ti* in Cypriot. (He also adduced evidence from Etruscan, just to confuse right with wrong reasoning!) If these guesses were right, then consonant 8 on the grid must be *n* and vowel 1 must be *i*, which automatically meant that Υ was *ni*, according to the grid.

Ventris's next step was inspired: a 'leap in the dark' of the kind mentioned by Chadwick (see the Introduction). He decided to pursue his February hunch about the names of Cretan towns, and see where the hypothesis would lead him.

The town of Amnisos, being the ancient port of Knossos, he knew was likely to be mentioned in the tablets. But Amnisos was its classical Greek name. Its name at the time when it was written syllabically in Linear B would, Ventris proposed, be *A-mi-ni-so*, with no final *s* – the 's' being the classical Greek ending also found, as we saw before, in the later Cypriot script. (Evans had had the same idea about Linear B spelling when he speculatively equated Linear B 'polo' with classical Greek 'pōlos'.) In introducing this assumption, that Linear B spelling might have omitted final *s* in nouns, Ventris was undoubtedly sticking out his neck, since he had no supporting linguistic evidence at all for such a spelling change between archaic Greek and classical Greek – but he plunged on.

Written in Linear B, A-mi-ni-so would be:

$$Υ - ? - Υ - ?$$

The first word in one 'triplet' was Τ Ϸ Υ ϒ. If it meant Amnisos, then

$$Ϸ = mi \qquad\qquad ϒ = so$$

Then, according to the grid, consonant 9 must be *m*, and vowel 2 must be *o*. This would mean, in turn (the so-called 'chain-reaction') that 𝍦 = *no*.

The first word in another 'triplet' was 𝍦 ϒ. Using the grid, this transliterated as *?-no-so*. If 𝍦 = *ko*, the name could be Knossos itself. In due course Ventris was to extract from the five 'triplets' the names of three further known Cretan towns:

    𐀶𐀪𐀰   *Tu-li-so* (Tulissos)

    𐀞𐀂𐀵   *Pa-i-to* (Phaistos)

    𐀷𐀑𐀵   *Lu-ki-to* (Luktos)

An entire 'triplet' could now be transliterated as:

    𐀀𐀖𐀛𐀰   *A-mi-ni-so* (Amnisos)

    𐀀𐀖𐀛𐀯𐀍   *A-mi-ni-si-jo* (Amnisian men)

    𐀀𐀖𐀛𐀯𐀊   *A-mi-ni-si-ja* (Amnisian women)

These proposed meanings of the second and third words, though as yet unproven by Ventris, reminded him of words with similar inflections in Homeric Greek, and were therefore promising. It looked as if Kober's 'triplets' were *not*, after all, noun declensions but something similar to the 'alternative name endings' he had originally proposed back in 1948: proper names of towns and their ethnica (e.g. London/Londoners, Paris/Parisians).

Thus proper names, vital in the Egyptian hieroglyphic decipherment, now looked as if they would prove to be vital in deciphering Linear B too. Instead of Ptolemy and Cleopatra, there was Amnisos and Knossos. But everything was still speculative, dependent on the initial assumptions for the phonetic values.

Having worked out various other 'Greek'-looking words in the tablets, Ventris was unable to contain himself. On 1 June, he sat down to type what would turn out to be his final Work Note, number 20, and boldly titled it: 'Are the Knossos and Pylos tablets written in Greek?' At the beginning, he called the short, five-page note 'a frivolous digression', 'not intended to prejudice' the serious analysis of the newly published Knossos tablets. Then he gave the exciting evidence about the Cretan town names and a handful of other words. At the end, he cautiously 'covered' himself: 'If pursued, I suspect that this line of decipherment would sooner or later come to an impasse, or dissipate itself in absurdities; and that it would be necessary to revert to the hypothesis of an indigenous, non-Indo-European language.... But this fantasy may be the excuse for us once more to ask ourselves the question: Which is historically more incongruous, a Knossos which writes Greek, or a Mycenae which writes "Cretan"?' During the next year, the Knossos, Pylos, Mycenae and other Linear B tablets would be compelled to deliver up an incontrovertible answer.

6
Breakthrough

'During the last couple of days I have been carrying on with the fantasy I discussed in my last Note; and though it runs completely counter to everything I've said in the past, I'm now almost completely convinced that the...tablets are in GREEK.'

Michael Ventris in a letter to Sir John Myres, mid-June 1952

We cannot speak of a precise instant of breakthrough when Ventris deciphered Linear B and revealed its secrets – as when Howard Carter's candle suddenly illuminated Tutankhamun's concealed tomb. But neither was the crucial insight a long drawn-out process. The key period was undoubtedly two or three weeks in late May and early June 1952. Lois Ventris, Michael's wife, remembered being woken by him in bed in the Highpoint flat at about 2 a.m. 'with a long story about place names like Amnisos and symbols for chariots and so on, all of course with illustrations'. In early June, there was another memorable moment. It happened when the Ventrises invited to dinner an architect friend, Michael Smith, and his South African-born wife Prudence, a post-war classics student at Somerville College, Oxford (where she had attended the famous and eccentric lectures of Sir John Myres), who in 1952 was a BBC radio producer. These two knew Ventris as a skilful and hard-working architect when he was at the Ministry of Education, who also had a 'hobby', the Minoan scripts, which they regarded as his amusement – 'rather as, at Somerville, it had seemed rather amusing that the brilliant philosopher Iris Murdoch should be "trying" to write a novel,' Prudence Smith wrote in a lively memoir finished just before her death in 1999.

That evening, for what seemed to her a very long time, she, her architect husband and Lois Ventris sat chatting on the Breuer furniture in the main room at 47 Highpoint, getting a little hungry and drunk on sherry while waiting for Michael, with Lois apologizing somewhat anxiously for his absence at fairly frequent intervals. He was in the study, she said, and would come out as soon as he could. Eventually, he burst into the room, his normally neat hair ruffled, 'full of apologies but even more full of excitement'. 'I know it, I *know* it. I am certain of it,' he told them.

After dinner, Michael took Prudence into the study. During the previous year, he had shown her some of the Work Notes as he had written them, and so she was able, to some extent at least, to follow the complicated business of vowel frequencies, syllabic spellings, inflectional endings and cross-references to other ancient languages in other ancient scripts, and the phonetic values set out on the various grids – which she nevertheless found 'as challenging, in their own way, as the Minoan labyrinth to its victims'. But she hung on listening to him, for even though she knew little about the Ventris methodology, she knew enough Greek not to doubt that if his complex positionings and suppositions were valid, then the revealed language was indeed a form of Greek. '[His] work still had a long way to go, but the road he had travelled entirely persuaded me, on that strange evening, of his achievement.'

Within days of the ruined dinner party, Ventris felt confident enough to write to Myres and Bennett – the two leading scholars in Linear B studies. 'Dear Sir John.... During the last couple of days I have been carrying on with the fantasy I discussed in my last Note [Work Note 20]; and though it runs completely counter to everything I've said in the past, I'm now almost completely convinced that the Pylos tablets are in GREEK. It's a pity there's not a new language to study, but it looks as if we must go to Linear A for that.' Then he listed a series of words and phrases with his proposed Greek transliterations and English translations, glossing some of them with explanations, and finished up: 'It may still be a hallucination, and you may well say that the Knossos forms just don't fit. But the thing that staggers me is that whenever I go to the Greek dictionary to check a word I seem to have found but which is unfamiliar to me, it generally seems to exist and to make sense.' To Bennett, the list of words he sent was longer and the explanation extremely terse: 'I have, I think, great news for you. You must judge for yourself, but I think I've deciphered Linear B, and that Knossos and Pylos are both in *Greek*.' Apart from a lengthy list of tablet numbers with his transliterations of their inscriptions in Greek, the only other evidence in the letter was a grid dated 18 June 1952, with 10 consonants and 5 vowels labelled with their phonetic values and more than 40 Linear B signs placed on it (see opposite).

At the same time, Prudence Smith, conscious of having an intellectual scoop on her hands, was persuading her colleagues at the BBC's highbrow Third Programme that Ventris must give a talk on his discovery. 'No, I had to tell them, he did not work in a university, or a museum, he happened to be a friend…a young architect. They were sceptical – rightly so, for I too was very young; but they gave in, I suppose, to my fervour.' She also had to persuade Ventris himself. For if he was wrong, he would not only make a fool of himself (like the Czech scholar Hrozný who had claimed to decipher several undeciphered scripts, including Linear B, in the 1940s), he would also discredit his methodology. But since his whole purpose in circulating the Work Notes to other scholars had been to open up discussion on the Minoan scripts, and since he knew that a scholarly exposition of his Greek theory in a journal might easily take a year or two to develop and publish (if it was accepted at all), Ventris too agreed to the talk.

'Deciphering Europe's earliest scripts' was broadcast on the BBC on 1 July – astonishingly soon after Ventris's breakthrough. It is the only

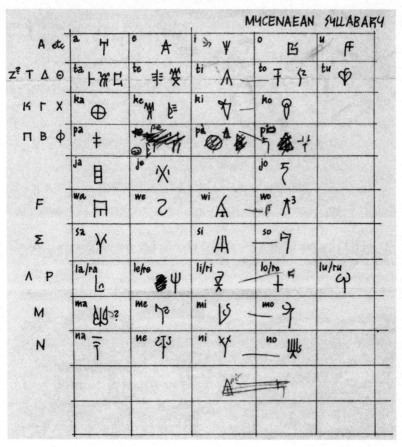

Ventris's Mycenaean syllabary, as sent to Emmett Bennett Jr in June 1952, with Bennett's pencilled emendations.

recording we have of his voice: urbane, clear, unemotional and precise, as one might expect, but also a curious combination of firmness and diffidence, reflecting the brilliant but still unproven nature of his discovery, and probably betraying something deeper too. In the most quoted passage, Ventris declared: 'For a long time I, too, thought that Etruscan might afford the clue we were looking for, but during the last few weeks, I have come to the conclusion that the Knossos and Pylos tablets must, after all, be written in Greek – a difficult and archaic Greek, seeing that it is 500 years older than Homer and written in a rather abbreviated form, but Greek nevertheless.' And this in turn meant, Ventris concluded the broadcast, that the language of the Linear B tablets from Knossos, like those from Pylos on mainland Greece, should no longer be referred to as 'Minoan' but as 'Mycenaean Greek' – that is, as the language not of Evans's Minoans but of the mainland Greek civilization based at Mycenae that had preceded the civilization of the classical Greeks.

The talk was a masterly exposition of complex, rarefied material for a non-specialist audience – and also, to quote its producer Prudence Smith, 'an essay in modesty' which even managed to preserve the speaker's 'rather surprised and grateful air of...a revelation which had somehow or other happened to him.' Old Myres wrote encouragingly afterwards to Ventris who replied that the ending had to be rewritten four times, 'starting from a decidedly Etruscan bias!' The single serious failing (which hardly anyone listening would have noticed) was that he omitted to mention Alice Kober – the scholar whose work had influenced Ventris the most – while he gave credit to many others, including of course Evans, Myres and Bennett. In his moment of triumph, even Michael Ventris was not above the innate human tendency to downplay the contribution of a rival, though in all his subsequent writings he seems to have realized his lack of generosity and given Kober her due.

There can be hardly any doubt that Kober, had she still been living in July 1952, would have treated Ventris's decipherment with scathing scepticism. Myres, though he may have been positive about the BBC talk, did not endorse Ventris's chief conclusion, neither did Bennett. Both scholars would take many months to come round to it; a solid consensus in favour of the decipherment would require two or three years to develop; and a few serious scholars would never accept it and would even revile it (as we shall see). Something similar happened with Champollion's decipherment of Egyptian hieroglyphs in 1823, which was not fully accepted until the 1860s; and again, in our own time, with the decipherment of Mayan glyphs started in the early 1950s, which was the subject of acrimonious debate for two or three decades and is yet to make it into some reference books.

To persuade the 'experts', three fundamental obstacles had somehow to be overcome by Ventris in July 1952, as he moved into the 'substitution' phase of the decipherment. First, he had to explain how he had arrived in a logical way at his phonetic values for the Linear B signs. Second, he had to show that 'Mycenaean' Greek related to classical Greek in a way that was both internally consistent throughout the Pylos and Knossos tablets and also consistent with the reconstructions of earlier, simpler forms of Greek made by classical philologists according to linguistic 'laws' governing sound changes over time and place. Third, he had to show how the many awkward words he had transliterated into forms which were *not* found in Greek dictionaries, might be interpreted plausibly as Greek.

On the first question, we already know from the previous chapter that Ventris was only partly successful. He could never completely justify his thought processes during the analysis phase of the decipherment, precisely because some of them were *not* logical but intuitive. Those who supported the decipherment were inclined to overlook this, and to argue that it was not the methods that mattered but the end result: did the phonetic values produce recognizable Greek words? If so, never mind how the values were arrived at – to put the argument baldly. But in dealing with the second and third questions, Ventris would be substantially successful over the next months and years, having taken the help of specialist scholars.

The first thing he did was to draw up a long vocabulary for Mycenaean Greek, showing all the words he had been able to interpret, including proper names like Amnisos, Knossos and Pylos. Overleaf is the first page (which does not show any proper names).

Let us have a look at a mere five words in his list:

a.   Number 7, *pa-te* in Mycenaean Greek, is equivalent to 'patēr' (father)

EXPERIMENTAL MYCENAEAN VOCABULARY 7.52

SIGNGROUPS ARE FROM PYLOS 1939 UNLESS PREFIXED BY K

#	K	signs	transliteration	gram.	Greek	gloss
1			da-mo	ds	δάμωι	community
2			da-ko-Ro	np	} λαικροί ?	carvers ?
3			da-ko-Ro-i	np		
4			da-ma-te	np	λάμαρτες	[see ...]
5			pa-Ro	PREP.	παρὸ +dat	= παρά ?
6	K		pa-te	np.m	πάντες	all
7			pa-te	ns	πατήρ	father
8			pa-te-de	ns	πατήρ λέ	but her father.....
9			pa-si	dp	πᾶσι	to all
10	K		pa-si-te-o-i	np	πᾶσι-θεοῖς ?	
11			pa-Ra-jo	ns.m	παλαιός ?	old
12			pa-Ra-ja	np.f	παλαιαί	,,
13	K		pa-we-a	np	φάϝεα	lights
14			pa-ka-na	np	σφαγναί ?	swords
15			te-u-ta-Ra-ko-Ro	ns	τεύτλαγροϛ	beetroot land
16			te-me-no	ns	τέμενος	area of corn-land
17			te-Re-ta	ns	τηρητάς	guardian
			[OR: τελεστάς			official ?]
				np	τηρηταί	,,
18			to-Re-ta-o	gp	τηρητάων	,,
19			te-o		τήως	for the meanwhile
			[OR: θεῶι ?]			
20			te-o-jo	gs	θεοῖο	of the god
21			te-ko-to-na-pe	ns	} τέκτων ἀπη- ?	wainwright ?
22			te-ko-to-a-pe	ns		
23	K		te-ko-to-ne		τέκτονες	carpenters
24	K		te-mi-••	ns.n	τερμιόϝεν ?	edged; bordered ?
25	K		te-mi-••-te	ds.n	τερμιόϝεντει	,,
26	K		te-mi-••-ta	np.n	τερμιόϝεντα	,,
			te-Re-te-we	np	-ϝεϛ	guardians? fosterparents
27	K		to-Ro-no-wo-ko		θρονοϝοργό-	chair-maker
28			to-Ro-qe-jo-me-no		τροϝειόμενο-	changed ?
29			to-to	ns.n	τότο	this
30			to-so	ns.mn	τόσσος, τόσσον	so much
31			to-so-jo	gs.m	τόσσοιο	,,
			to-so	np.m	τόσσοι	so many
32			to-so-de		τοσσόϛε, τοσσοίϛε	
33			to-sa	np.f	τόσσαι	,,
34			to-sa-de	,,	τοσσαίϛε	,,
35			to-jo-qe	gs.m	τοῖό ϝε	and of the —
36			to-ko-so-wo-ko	np.m	τοξοϝοργοί	bow-makers
37			to-ko-do-mo	np.m	τοιχολόμοι	builders
38			na-u-do-mo		ναυλόμο-	ship-builder
39			di-do-si	3s.pr	λιλόσι	they give
40			di-wi-ja	ns.f	λιϝια	excellent; 1st class
41			di-pte-Ra-po-Ro	np	λιφθεραφόροι	[a trade]
42			a-Ro-u-Ra		ἀρουρα-	corn-land
43			a-pa-Re-u-si	dp	ἀσκαλῠσι	fishermen
44			a-to-po-qo	np	ἀρτοπόϙοι	bakers
45			a-to-mo	ns	ἀρθμός	league
46			a-to-mo-i	np	ἀρθμοί	,,
47	K		a-na-mo-to	ns.n	ἀνάρμοστον	not fitted out

The first page of Ventris's Mycenaean vocabulary list, July 1952.

in classical Greek. Final '-r' is omitted in Mycenaean Greek; and the length of vowels is not noted (contrast classical Greek which has both epsilon, ε, for 'e', and eta, η, for 'ē').

b. Number 14, *pa-ka-na*, is equivalent to 'phasgana' (swords). (Ventris originally gave a somewhat different equivalent word.) There is no aspirated 'p', *ph*, so the classical Greek phi, φ, is represented simply by the inherent consonant 'p', e.g. the classical Greek syllable 'pha-' is written with the sign for *pa*; the script does not distinguish between *k* and *g*; and 's' is omitted when before another consonant (in this case 'g').

c. Number 17, *te-re-ta*, is equivalent to 'telestās' (official). The script does not distinguish *r* and *l* (like Japanese, which is why Japanese speakers tend to pronounce 'r' and 'l' the same when speaking English – hence the familiar joke about 'flied lice'); and again 's' is omitted when before another consonant (in this case 't') and also when final (compare *A-mi-ni-so* = Amnisos).

d. Number 23, *te-ko-to-ne*, is equivalent to 'tektones' (carpenters). The stop consonant 'k', when it precedes another consonant (in this case 't'), is generally written with the vowel of the following syllable (in this case 'o'); and again, final '-s' is omitted.

e. Number 30, *to-so*, is equivalent to 'tossos' (so much). This is the 'total' word on the tablets 𐀵 𐀰 (see pages 24–25). Double consonants are not distinguished; and yet again, 's' is omitted when final.

These examples suggest a rather loose way of spelling in Mycenaean Greek, and there are quite a number of other spelling rules that have not yet been mentioned. For instance, the script does not distinguish *p* and *b* (in addition to *ph*) – thus the two signs which were read *pa-te* in number 7 above could also theoretically be read *pha-te* and *ba-te*. A second rule concerns diphthongs, where the second component is in some cases indicated (as in *ai, eu, ou*) and in other cases generally omitted (as in *a(i), e(i), o(i), u(i)*), except before another vowel (e.g. classical Greek '-aios') and in the initial sign *ai*. A third rule is the glide that intervenes in pronunciation between an *i* and a following vowel, which is generally indicated in Mycenaean by 'j' – hence Kober's 'triplet' (page 69) *A-mi-ni-so* (Amnisos)/ *A-mi-ni-si-jo* (Amnisian men)/*A-mi-ni-si-ja* (Amnisian women) – which in classical Greek would be written without the 'j' and pronounced with a glide: Amnisos/Amnis**ioi**/Amnis**iai**.

This quick tour of the spelling rules is intended mainly to show what Ventris was up against, without confusing the reader with too much tricky detail. It is not necessary to understand the Mycenaean spelling rules to grasp Ventris's achievement, but we need to realize that the looseness of the rules made the decipherment an easy target for unsympathetic critics, especially in its early stages when the rules had not been fully formulated. Yet as Ventris and Chadwick pointed out in their first joint writing, 'If the language is Greek, we are seeing it at a stage 1000 years older than Plato (a difference in date as great as between Beowulf and Shakespeare), and separated from the classical idiom by a Dark Age. It is set in a different environment, and surrounded, possibly closely inter-mingled, with barbarian languages spoken by peoples of equal or superior culture. Some elements of the vocabulary may be either "Aegean", or dis-torted by non-Greek scribes, or part of an older stratum of Greek unfamilar to classical philology.'

It is at this point, in mid-July 1952, that John Chadwick enters the Linear B story as a contributor to the decipherment. From his specialized knowledge of archaic Greek dialects, his wider interest in languages and his experience of wartime code-breaking, he would now help Ventris sort out, with admirable clarity, what was and what was not reasonable in interpreting the Mycenaean word formations tumbling out of the tablets.

Chadwick had recently been appointed as a junior lecturer in classical philology at Cambridge University, but he had yet to move to Cambridge and was still living in Oxford where he worked on the *Oxford Latin Dictionary*. (Before that, he had studied classics at Cambridge and served during the war at Bletchley Park, specializing in the translation of decrypted Japanese naval messages sent to Tokyo from Berlin.) For some time, he had been toying with Linear B, without making any progress, and without any knowledge of Ventris and his Work Notes, to his later chagrin. So when he heard the BBC broadcast on 1 July, he immediately contacted Myres, copied down the proposed phonetic values from the latest grid and began to apply them to the published tablets. Within a few days, despite the old man's scepticism and his own instinctive cautiousness, Chadwick was an enthusiastic and confident convert. He was the first scholar to be won over by the decipherment, because he had the philological training to make sense of the results, which was not true of Bennett or Myres. On 9 July, he told the latter bluntly: 'I think we must accept the fact that a new chapter in Greek history, philology and epigraphy is about to be written.'

A slightly grudging Myres gave Ventris Chadwick's address and vice versa, and during July, a correspondence rapidly got going between them. A few excerpts are worth quoting for their flavour of what Chadwick would later call 'very fruitful cooperation' – 'group working' under another name – reminiscent of his own analogy with Holmes and Watson, mentioned in the Introduction.

Ventris wrote first, on 9 July, enclosing some notes, 'as I gather you have been working for some time on the same problem.... If you find any points of contact between your work and mine it would be very interesting to have the opportunity of exchanging views.'

Chadwick, replying on 13 July, opened by offering his congratulations on 'having solved the Minoan problem; it is a magnificent achievement and you are yet only at the beginning of your triumph.' He concluded: 'If there is anything a mere philologist can do, please let me know. I shall go ahead trying to unravel the tablets on the basis of your solution, and will let you know if I find anything helpful.'

Ventris responded by return at length: 'Frankly at the moment I feel rather in need of moral support. The whole issue is getting to the stage where a lot of people will be looking at it very sceptically, and I am conscious there's a lot which so far can't be very satisfactorily explained. There's a kind of central area of sense, but still a great periphery which is baffling...I've been feeling the need of a "mere philologist" to keep me on the right lines.... It would be extremely useful to me if I could count on your help, not only in trying to make sense of the material, but also in drawing the conclusions about the [word] formations in terms of dialect and stage of development. I sounded *JHS* [the *Journal of Hellenic Studies*], who had asked me to review *Scripta Minoa*, if they would have room for an article on "Mycenaean Greek" in next year's number, for which the MS would be in by the end of November.... If they do, and if the vocabulary can be solidified some more by then, then would you be willing to collaborate in this article?' In a PS, Ventris added that he was worried by the absence of the definite article (present in classical Greek) in Mycenaean Greek.

Chadwick wrote back on 17 July: 'I am not surprised you are meeting with some resistance; the idea is too staggering to swallow at once.... [But] being a philologist I am not in the least worried by inexplicable words, as there are plenty in much later inscriptions, or by curious spellings and survivals. A further point is that I am familiar with Japanese, which uses to supplement the Chinese ideograms [logograms] a syllabary very similar in form to the Cypriot, and of course lacking signs for L: e.g. Apollo appears as *a-po-ro*.... The definite article ought not to be present, as it is not yet fully developed in Homer...I should have been much more worried if you *had* found an article.' He welcomed the chance to collaborate.

On 21 July, Ventris told Chadwick: 'I see that you will be a very valuable ally'. He enclosed a set of Work Notes with a frank appraisal of their successes and failures. Replying on 25 July, Chadwick worried about infringing Ventris's copyright, so to speak, by showing his grid to other scholars. But Ventris unsurprisingly encouraged him on 28 July: 'I don't feel very strong copyright in the suggested solution, because every other day I get so doubtful about the whole thing that I'd almost rather it was someone else's. In fact, I'd like as many people as possible to be thinking about the problem on these lines, as there are so many loose ends still dangling: and if I come to write up some of the approach in an article, it will be useful to have had as much informed comment as possible beforehand.'

His diffidence was not false modesty; he really felt it. His letters to Myres and Bennett at this time are riddled with the same doubt. No wonder he was tickled to read a news report about Charlie Chaplin's controversial return to London from America, which he passed on without comment to Myres. Asked by a reporter about his next film, Chaplin said: 'I intend to make a picture about New York. It will be about a Displaced Person arriving in the New World. He will be suffering from a head wound which has given him the complaint called cryptosthenia, whereby he speaks in an ancient language. No one can understand him at the immigration barriers, and so he is allowed to pass all the language tests.' Then Chaplin mimed a scene as he imagined it at the questioning point and said: 'Effelequesta' – 'They think that's Greek.'

Ventris was sharply conscious that he himself was some sort of alien arriving in the world of academe speaking a possibly imaginary language that purported to be Greek. With this feeling at the forefront of his mind, over the summer of 1952 he wrote the first draft of what would become one of the most important (and best-selling) papers ever published by the venerable *Journal of Hellenic Studies*, cautiously entitled 'Evidence for Greek dialect in the Mycenaean archives'.

In late September, he sent it to Chadwick with the comment: 'the first duty seems to be to supply the reasoning behind the interpretation, and the kind of popularization which tries to draw historical conclusions from the material can only come after.' In other words, the justification of the decipherment must be the main purpose of the article, not a discussion of what the tablets might tell the world about more glamorous subjects such as King Minos, Homer and the Trojan war. The draft also went to Bennett and Myres (its complex signs neatly copied on to carbons by Ventris – no photocopying in 1952!). 'The introduction has been one of the hardest parts to write, both in giving a fair view of the historical background, and in striking a balance between over-optimism and over-timidity in presenting what we feel is a very considerable body of pro-Greek evidence', Ventris told Myres. 'If anything, it will be Chadwick who will be for stating the proposition in more unequivocal terms.'

This last was true, but Chadwick also turned out to be a stern critic of 'over-optimism' that might appear to be linguistic legerdemain. Bearing in mind that most *JHS* readers were knowledgeable only about classical Greek, not the Greek of the earlier dialects, he told Ventris: 'Half of the article will consist of incomprehensible references and the other half of unwarranted assumptions.' Soon afterwards, in mid-October, the two men met in Cambridge for the first time to discuss the problem – a meeting followed by a Swissair postcard from Ventris, postmarked Gstaad and purely about Linear B; personal matters would seldom intrude in their correspondence. A second draft by Ventris in early November fared little better with Chadwick: 'I think a lot of your suggestions are brilliant, and many may well prove right. But I think you are trying to go too far at once; if I may repeat what I said before, one should be cautious but not timid. In particular I feel that one should be very careful to show that proper linguistic laws are in operation, and be wary of varying the rules to suit peculiar cases.'

The impact of all this criticism was to reduce the section on the decipherment itself to less than two pages out of twenty, and instead to focus on giving large amounts of Mycenaean vocabulary, which ordinary classicists would grasp more easily than Ventris's 'brilliance'. Having examined these Ventris/Chadwick transliterations/translations of certain sign groups in the tablets, other scholars could then substitute the phonetic values from the grid into Linear B sign groups of their own choosing, and make their own convincing discoveries. Although Chadwick was probably right in his tactical advice to Ventris, it did have the effect (as Chadwick later admitted) of depriving us of a fuller account of the decipherment at the time when this was freshest in Ventris's mind. In the end, Ventris never wrote such an account.

Of the hundreds of results presented in this article, two were particularly striking. The first was an exceptionally long name containing eight signs, which could be transliterated with the sign list as *E-te-wo-ke-re-we-i-jo* – an exact fit (according to the spelling rules) with a patronymic derived from the classical Greek name Eteocles in what we know was its ancestral form. Since there are 200,000 million possible permutations of eight syllables, coincidence was ruled out here. The second result was a tablet from Knossos that Ventris later described as 'the most startling document...for a generation brought up to regard Knossos as the preserve of Evans's Great Mother Goddess'. It contained four names recognizable as ancient *Greek* divine names: *A-ta-na* (Athena), *E-nu-wa-ri-jo* (Enyalios – Ares), *Pa-ja-wo* (Homeric Paiēōn – Paian or Apollo) and *Po-se-da[-o]* (Poseidon). (The square bracket indicates that the tablet is broken here.) 'I've a rooted objection to finding gods' names on the tablets', Ventris told Chadwick, because cranky decipherers so often resorted to religion to explain undeciphered scripts (and besides, Ventris was atheistically inclined). The transliteration looked 'too good to be true'. Agreed about 'the danger of finding divine names', replied Chadwick, 'but if we have them I would much rather have four on one tablet than find them scattered about in unverifiable contexts.' They eventually accepted that the four Greek gods' names were genuine, and the tablet probably recorded the dedication of one item of something unknown to each of the four gods (the numeral 1 appeared on the tablet, apparently next to each name).

In late November, the joint article was at last despatched to the journal for typesetting (though it would not appear in print until the late summer of 1953). Ventris thanked Chadwick for making an 'enormous difference to its value and cogency'. Neither Myres nor Bennett had contributed, despite being invited to do so. 'It obviously is a bit hard for an old man to be told that Greek has been sitting under his nose for 40-50 years without his suspecting it', Ventris remarked to Chadwick. To Bennett he wrote: 'As far as we are concerned the line of attack is common knowledge among our band of sleuths now, and there's no reason why the discussion shouldn't be general and battle be joined as from now.'

At this point, near the end of 1952, nothing about the decipherment had appeared in public except the BBC talk, but Ventris was receiving requests for articles, talks and interviews, as was Chadwick. *The Times* asked Ventris to write a piece, but he declined because he did not want to rehash the BBC talk or anticipate the *Journal of Hellenic Studies* article, or 'drag you Siamese-twin fashion into publicity which may be badly timed', he told Chadwick. Instead, he said, he had given *The Times* two pages of background and suggested that their New York correspondent try to contact Bennett for an opinion. 'I wish him luck.'

Bennett offered the following comment: 'I think there is not yet enough material available to make a deciphering of these tablets certain one way or the other. Michael Ventris's theory that the language of the Minoan tablets is a very early Greek is a tempting possibility. That is all I would say at this stage.' To Ventris himself, he wrote ironically, referring to his 'fine set of cautious, non-committal phrases'. But the truth was – as Bennett knew by now even though he was not ready to say so publicly – that Ventris's decipherment was correct, and he, Bennett, had missed the Linear B decipherment boat. Both he and Chadwick were equally cautious and excellent scholars, but Chadwick had the major advantage over Bennett of a sound linguistic training in early Greek. Bennett's disappointment at not having perceived the Greek solution before 1952 was however softened by the transparent originality, brilliance and modesty of Ventris himself; it would have been galling indeed for Bennett if Chadwick, or one of the other European scholars, had beaten him to the solution. He and Ventris would always remain on congenial terms: as personalities, they were actually more *simpatico* than Ventris and Chadwick – for one thing they shared a sense of humour, which was not Chadwick's strongest suit.

In Sweden, by contrast, a senior scholar at the University of Uppsala, Arne Furumark, had gone overboard for the decipherment in a major press announcement in November – the first on the Continent. An embarrassed Ventris tried to correct certain enthusiastic misstatements in interviews with the Swedish newspapers, and then passed on the cuttings to Chadwick and Bennett 'in their awful entirety' with his own translations for their benefit. 'How do you come to be so expert in Swedish?' replied Chadwick. 'But I have long ceased being surprised at the extent of your knowledge. It's a great pity you did not choose an academic career; but there are many things to be said against such a life.'

Rather than writing for newspapers, both men preferred to concentrate on persuading academics through private correspondence and talks at universities. In December, Chadwick lectured at Oxford. ('I looked in to see Sir John Myres.... He thinks you ought to abandon architecture and devote yourself wholly to Mycenaean!') In early May, Ventris spoke at Cambridge, where he met Chadwick for the second time, and afterwards received some advice from him about a forthcoming talk at Oxford: 'if I might make a suggestion I feel it would be appropriate...to be a little more definite in asserting the language to be Greek. A proper intellectual humility is a good thing, but (especially at Oxford) it may be mistaken for diffidence.' Ventris would never be very comfortable in the company of professional classicists.

However, big news that would push the decipherment into the headlines, whether Ventris wanted it there or not, was about to break. During 1952, the American archaeologist Carl Blegen (who had received Ventris's

Work Notes) had resumed his pre-war excavations in the 'Palace of Nestor' at Pylos, and the British archaeologist Alan Wace had excavated further at Mycenae. Both men had found fresh Linear B tablets: some 400 at Pylos, and about 40 at Mycenae. In March, Ventris had dinner with Blegen in London to encourage him to reveal what he had found. He reported to Chadwick: 'on the decipherment problem in general, [Blegen] feels the tablets ought to be in Greek, but proposes to be "neutral" until the decipherers get the answer finally sorted out.'

Two months later, in mid-May, he received a letter from Blegen in Athens. Immediately, instead of writing a letter as usual, Ventris phoned Chadwick at his flat in Cambridge, his voice brimming with excitement – 'he rarely showed signs of emotion, but for him this was a dramatic moment,' Chadwick recalled in *The Decipherment of Linear B*. Blegen had written: 'Since my return to Greece I have spent much of my time working on the tablets from Pylos, getting them ready to be photographed. I have tried your experimental syllabary on some of them.... Enclosed for your information is a copy of P641, which you may find interesting. It evidently deals with pots, some of three legs, some with four handles, some with three, and others without handles. The first word by your system seems to be *ti-ri-po-de* and it recurs twice as *ti-ri-po* (singular?). The four-handled pot is preceded by *qe-to-ro-we*, the three-handled by *ti-ri-wo-we* or *ti-ri-jo-we*, the handleless pot by *a-no-we*. All this seems too good to be true. Is coincidence excluded? The other words are not so easy to explain.'

Opposite is a photograph of tablet P641, with drawings by Ventris and transliterations into Mycenaean and translations into English by Ventris and Chadwick.

Even to the untrained eye, the match between the three-legged pictogram ⚏ and its accompanying word *ti-ri-po* (compare 'tripos', tripod cauldron, in classical Greek), is impressive. With some knowledge of Greek, the four-handled, three-handled and no-handled goblet

tiripode aikeu keresijo weke   2
(tripod cauldron of Cretan
workmanship of the *aikeu* type 2)

tiripo eme pode owowe   1
(tripod cauldron with a single handle
on one foot 1)

tiripo keresijo weke
(tripod cauldron of Cretan workmanship)

apu kekaumeno kerea
(burnt at the legs)

qeto   3
(wine jars 3)

dipa mezoe qetorowe   1
(larger-sized goblet with four handles 1)

dipae mezoe tiriowee   2
(larger-sized goblet with three handles 2)

dipa mewijo qetorowe   1
(smaller-sized goblet with four handles 1)

dipa mewijo tirijowe   1
(smaller-sized goblet with three handles 1)

dipa mewijo anowe   1
(smaller-sized goblet without a handle 1)

Tablet P641 with Ventris's own drawings, and transliterations by Ventris and Chadwick.

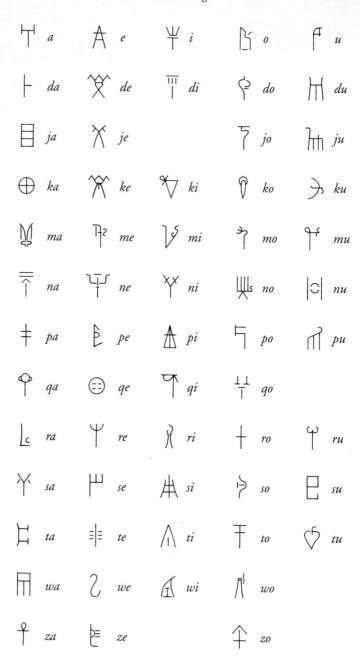

The basic *Linear B* syllabary.

pictograms accompanying *qe-to-ro-we*, *ti-ri-jo-we* and *a-no-we* are easily matched with 'tetra-' (four in classical Greek, but compare 'quattuor' in Latin), 'tri-' (three in classical Greek), and 'an-' (the negative prefix) – combined with *-o-we* ('-oues', ears/handles, in classical Greek). The words *me-zo* and *me-wi-jo* meaning 'larger' and 'smaller' respectively were already known from their use in classifying children into 'seniors' and 'juniors'. Another word, *di-pa*, had to be the vessel called 'depas' mentioned in Homer.

Was it too far-fetched to associate this four-handled goblet in King Nestor's palace archives with the cup described by Homer in the *Iliad*, before Nestor sets off for the Trojan war? It was 'a magnificent cup adorned with golden studs.... It had four handles.... Anyone else would have found it difficult to shift the cup from the table when full, but Nestor, old as he was, could lift it without trouble.' At any rate, when Ventris published his above drawing of the tablet and its signs, he provocatively entitled his article, 'King Nestor's four-handled cups'. (I possess a copy he signed for his former classics master Patrick Hunter, who gave it to me not long before he died.)

Ventris called P641 'a sort of Rosetta stone'. Chadwick wrote: 'I do not see how even the most sceptical can find cause to doubt this.' Bennett admitted: 'Looks hard to beat! and I thoroughly understand Blegen's and your excitement.' The tablet immediately became the *pièce de résistance* in all lectures given by Ventris or Chadwick.

On 24 June 1953, Ventris spoke at the Society of Antiquaries at Burlington House in London, the very place in which he had first seen a Linear B tablet back in 1936 as a 14-year-old. The following day, *The Times* carried a report and – a rare honour for a scholarly discovery – also devoted a leader article, 'On the threshold?', to the talk. 'Mr Ventris is scrupulous not to encourage extravagant hopes. Yet imagination cannot restrain itself from speculating on the possible enlargement of our historic horizons if the thalassocrats of three or four thousand years ago should prove able after all to communicate with us in a language that we know.... Shall we some day come upon the relics of that long succession of forgotten poets who must surely have shaped and tuned the sonorous organ of the Greek speech, as it must have been shaped and tuned through many generations to be capable of "the surge and thunder of the *Odyssey*"? The questions will not be silenced. All we have at present is a dozen doubtful words picked out of some magnate's household books. But it is the first step that counts.' Next to the leader was a piece entitled 'At the summit of Everest', by its climber Edmund Hillary. The coincidence was too much, and the decipherment was quickly dubbed 'the Everest of Greek archaeology' – to the considerable embarrassment of the decipherer.

Chadwick was unable to be there for the talk, so Ventris described to him the enthusiastic reaction, with 'invidious comparisons to Everest!' but the Greek ambassador looking '*extremely* somnolent, poor chap.' The chief critic of the decipherment, Arthur Beattie, professor of Greek at Edinburgh University, attended too. According to Ventris, Beattie 'swallowed the tripods and went away good-naturedly complaining that "this must be the most irregular writing system on record".' (In fact, he would remain virulently critical, as we shall see.) As for the *Times* leader, Ventris found it a bit 'fanciful' for his taste, and for once he regretted that it played down the concrete results: 'Still it's a historic page with "The summit of Everest"; and, additional coincidence, the announcement of my sister-in-law's engagement. All three things we have struggled for for many years!' (By way of celebrating a whole year of correspondence and collaboration, he now suggested that Chadwick and he move to Christian names and call each other John and Michael.)

Other papers picked up the story. One tabloid commented that Ventris 'looks as though he would be more at home in a university rowing eight than probing the mystery of an unknown language', while another had the same impression but preferred a rugger scrum. The *Architects'*

Ventris at work on Linear B.

Journal noted: 'It was pleasant to discover a *Times* leader the other day on architect Michael Ventris's hobby – if that is not too flippant a word – of breaking the Minoan code. On this subject, which has been a world mystery since the time of Sir Arthur Evans, Michael Ventris gave an interesting broadcast last year; but a *Times* leader being in the nature of a Papal Bull, the last doubt has now been removed.' Celebrity this was not – even by the pre-television standards of 1953. But the name Michael Ventris was now known not merely to a small group of classical scholars and architects but to hundreds of thousands of educated people in Britain – and soon in the United States and across Europe too.

Yet although Ventris, with Chadwick's aid, had certainly taken more than the 'first step' mentioned by *The Times*, there were still formidable problems with the decipherment. Even the 'tripods' tablet, P641, contained contradictions and mysterious words, some of which scholars are still arguing over today. (We shall scrutinize one of the phrases in the next chapter.) 'I'm only too conscious that Linear B is only one-quarter deciphered, at best; or that, if technically "deciphered", we still can't read the tablets extensively – which from the layman's point of view isn't much better', Ventris confessed to Bennett, appending to his letter a passage about the difficult early days of Champollion's decipherment taken from the German book on Egyptian hieroglyphs he had read as a young boy. The big task now, as he saw it, was to work with Chadwick and a growing number of others on a thorough-going study of the tablets that would convince even the most sceptical of minds that Linear B really could be read.

7

Documents in Mycenaean Greek

"Not quite the Greek you taught me, I'm afraid!"
Inscription by Michael Ventris on his first post-decipherment publication
sent to his former classics master, autumn 1953

'I'm spending most of my time scrubbing floors at the new house at the moment', Ventris told Chadwick at the end of August 1953. Three weeks later he, Lois and their two young children Nikki and Tessa, taking their Breuer furniture with them, moved into 19 North End, the modest but well-built house he had designed in the spring and summer of 1952 in a leafy private corner of Hampstead, just off the Heath. The long years at Highpoint – with their mixed memories of school holidays, his late mother Dorothea, the war, marriage, student years as an architect, and endless poring over Linear B until he finally 'cracked' it – were over. A fresh phase was beginning in his life, both personally and with regard to the decipherment.

'Evidence for Greek dialect in the Mycenaean archives', written with Chadwick in late 1952, had just been published by the *Journal of Hellenic Studies*. Of course, a lot had happened in the nine months since the joint article was submitted in November, but this was the first solid scholarly exposition of the decipherment to appear in print and there was a rush for it among classicists and others – so much so that the paper was reprinted as a separate pamphlet and sold more than a thousand copies. Also, the hundreds of new tablets excavated by Blegen at Pylos in 1952, and a rather smaller number discovered by Wace at Mycenae, were about to become available for scrutiny (until now Ventris had seen only the celebrated 'tripods' tablet sent by Blegen in May). These tablets were virgin material, quite unknown pre-decipherment. Therefore they ought to provide an excellent check on the validity of Ventris's phonetic values. Now the third and last phase of the decipherment, following the analysis phase (up to June 1952) and the substitution phase (June 1952 to mid-1953), could begin in earnest.

In the intellectual world, the ultimate test of an idea's worth and the measure of one's success in proposing it, is that professionals respond and begin to include the idea in their work – whether by incorporating it, rejecting it, or, more usually, by modifying it through sympathy mixed with scepticism. (Naturally credit is not always given to the original source!) From the middle of 1953 onwards, this was indeed the case with the Ventris decipherment. Scholars interested in the early Aegean scripts from across Europe and the United States quickly started to read Linear B. The overwhelming majority agreed that the script wrote a form of early Greek; but there was serious disagreement about how to interpret particular inscriptions. There were also various cranks and, as ever in archaeological decipherment, it was not always simple to discern who the cranks were. 'After the *Times* article I had a letter from a crank, enclosed', Ventris told Chadwick in July. 'I thought the only way to see what he was up to was to try him out on the TRIPODS. And a pretty good hash it is; I've now broken off the engagement. The trouble is that, ridiculous as his ideas are, one always has the uneasy feeling of "there, but for the grace of God..."; and one's worst nightmare is that one has oneself been a victim of a similar delusion.' Being an 'amateur', Ventris was quite sensitive on the point.

He was wryly amused by the nationalist slant of some reactions. A well-known Greek scholar wrote (in Ventris's translation): 'We Greeks owe many thanks to the foreign scholars who have applied themselves with remarkable devotion to the laborious work of solving the riddle of the script and language, in which are written the age-old records of our ancestors found in the sacred soil of our Fatherland.' While a Russian (again translated by Ventris) commented: 'The data from the Pylos and Knossos tablets completely support the interpretation followed by Soviet science of the slave-based character of Cretan and Mycenaean society...and once again refute the modernizing prejudices still present in the works of many bourgeois historians.'

It is never easy to define the point at which a script can be said to be 'deciphered'. Even with Egyptian hieroglyphic, there are words and passages which are almost totally obscure. When Linda Schele, a key figure in the Maya decipherment, was asked how much of the Mayan glyphs had been deciphered, she would always answer that it depended what you meant by 'deciphered'. In 1993, a few years before her early death, she wrote: 'Some glyphs can be translated exactly; we know the original word or its syllabic value. For other glyphs, we have the meaning (for example, we have evidence that a glyph means "to hold or grasp"), but we do not yet know the Mayan words. There are other glyphs for which we know the general meaning, but we haven't found the original word; for example, we may know it involves war, marriage, or perhaps that the event always occurs before age 13, but we cannot associate the glyph with a precise action. For others, we can only recover their syntactical function; for example, we may know a glyph occurs in the position of a verb, but we have no other information. To me the most frustrating state is to have a glyph with known phonetic signs, so that we can pronounce the glyph, but we cannot find the word in any of the Mayan languages. If a glyph is unique or occurs in only a few texts, we have little chance of translating it.'

Linear B suffers from similar difficulties, although it is definitely more fully deciphered than the Mayan script. Right from the start, there have been accusations that the spelling rules are so loose that Linear B sign groups can be manipulated to produce Greek words that in reality are not present in the tablets. As Ventris told Patrick Hunter, his former classics teacher at Stowe, when sending him a copy of his joint paper with Chadwick: 'Not quite the Greek you taught me, I'm afraid!' – a fine example of his exquisite, gentle irony.

To Bennett, at the same time he pointed out that in the Cypriot script the sign ⸱ (remember ⌐ †, *polo*, on page 36) can represent at least 15 different Greek syllables:

po	*bo*	*pho*
pon-	*bon-*	*phon-*
pom-	*bom-*	*phom-*
pō	*bō*	*phō*
p-	*b-*	*ph-*

Whereas in Linear B, he said, we might be faced with at least 39 alternatives (ˌ is the Greek iota):

po	*pō*	*bo*	*bō*	*pho*	*phō*
poi	*pǫ*	*boi*	*bǫ*	*phoi*	*phǫ*
pol	*pōn*	*bol*	*bōn*	*phol*	*phōn*
pom	*pōr*	*bom*	*bōr*	*phom*	*phōr*
pon	*pōs*	*bon*	*bōs*	*phon*	*phōs*
por		*bor*		*phor*	
pos	*p-*	*bos*	*b-*	*phos*	*ph-*

– each of which might be prefixed with an initial -*s*.

To explain the situation to outsiders – and at the many lectures he was now being asked to give – Ventris made a 'toy' out of cardboard (rather reminiscent of his simple model of a 'grid' which hung on the wall at Highpoint). It consisted of a box with little windows through which one could slide paper strips. Each movable strip corresponded to one Linear B syllabic sign and listed all its possible transliterations (written in Greek letters, rather than in roman script as above). The strips could then be slid up and down or inserted in the windows in a different order so as to create all possible spelling permutations of a given set of syllabic signs. Ventris added a sketch for Bennett's benefit, showing the four signs Λ𐃑𐃏𐃅 thought to spell the Greek word 'tiripod(e)', as featured in the famous 'tripods' tablet P641:

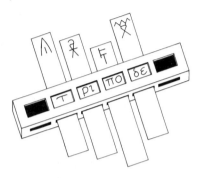

(Bennett, as a former wartime cryptographer, replied: 'I may try to make one of your toys. They are just the sort of thing I used to play with for the army so I will feel right at home.')

Soon, Bennett went to Greece in order to make drawings of the Pylos tablets discovered in 1952. From Athens he wrote ruefully, and perhaps a shade mischievously, to Ventris: 'I don't seem to invent inserted letters very easily or notice parallels in Greek, so that I will gladly let you do that end in time.' Back in England, Ventris and Chadwick waited anxiously. In December, Bennett generously mailed a partial set of drawings to Ventris, adding: 'I hope these will be of some use to you, and even more that you can enlighten me on them…. Once one starts putting values in the texts and looking up etymologies it is very hard to know when to stop. I have probably stayed too long on the other end of the job, but it also has to be done.'

The two collaborators decided on an experiment to test the validity of the decipherment. They would each, *independently* of the other, write detailed interpretations of the virgin Pylos tablets and mail them separately to Bennett in Athens. Only after doing so would they compare notes. Something similar had been attempted in 1857 (though neither Ventris nor Chadwick seems to have been conscious of the comparison), when four 'rival' scholars of cuneiform were asked by the Royal Asiatic Society to submit independent translations of a newly discovered inscription; this produced useful results at the early stage of the decipherment of Babylonian cuneiform.

In late January, Ventris fired off his interpretations: 29 closely typed pages minutely inscribed with Linear B in his trademark handwriting. Chadwick did the same, telling Bennett: 'I expect you will have some good laughs when you come to compare the different versions.' But the American scholar seems to have been stunned into silence by these two linguistic salvoes from England, contenting himself with a heartfelt thank you to Ventris for clarifying one particular sign group at long distance: 'I'd not have seen it otherwise.' The surface of the tablet in question was too damaged to identify the signs with any certainty, but Ventris's suggested reading, based on the meaning of the surrounding signs as read using his phonetic values, had led Bennett to 'see' what his eyes would otherwise have missed. In a way, it was an apt response from this ace epigrapher who was no great linguist. Observation had been suggested by theory, rather than the other way around, as happens quite often in science; for example in astronomy, the planet Pluto was first observed after its existence had been deduced from an analysis of perturbations in the orbit of Uranus and Neptune.

When Ventris and Chadwick eventually got together at North End for the weekend, they too were fairly satisfied. Their twin analyses of the new Pylos tablets shared much common ground. But they were also uneasily aware that there were considerable differences between their two interpretations. Plainly the decipherment still had a long way to go.

At this point, in early 1954, a sizeable group of British classicists clambered on board the Linear B bandwagon, with varying degrees of confidence. Leonard Palmer, the professor of classical philology at Oxford, was perhaps the cleverest of them; and he made sure that everyone knew it. He and Chadwick enjoyed a prickly relationship, in which *Professor* Palmer liked to refer ostentatiously to *Mr* Chadwick. There seems little doubt that in Palmer's view, 'Ventris and Palmer' would have been the appropriate combination for the history books, rather than Ventris and Chadwick. While there is no question that Palmer accepted the fundamental correctness of the decipherment and hugely admired Ventris personally, despite the architect's un-Oxonian diffidence, he would nevertheless be severely critical of some of his interpretations (while implying that the blame for these probably lay with Chadwick!).

A pioneering 'Minoan Linear B Seminar' was established at the newly founded Institute of Classical Studies in London, with the enthusiastic advocacy of a professor of Greek at University College, Tom Webster. Ventris agreed to lead the discussion at the first meeting in January and later gave a lecture which was attended by the king of Sweden; in fact he attended the regular seminars many times until the end of 1955. The finest classical scholars of the day came and lectured, and debated matters such as whether the Linear B sign group read as *po-ni-ke* referred to the fabulous phoenix bird or to the palm tree (both of which share the same spelling in classical Greek), and whether Homer had actually *seen* a 'depas' (cup) of the kind that only King Nestor could lift when it was full, or merely imagined it. Some of the arguments became very heated, but as a student participant, Ian Martin, recalled: 'Amidst the clash of conflicting egos, the one man without whose vision, insight, and determination not one single one of us would have been there, remained for the most part firmly silent.'

Ventris's reticence at the London seminars was generally construed as modesty, which was true enough. But he was also sensible to the need to keep his mouth shut. Before the seminar got going, he wrote to Chadwick: 'I feel these chaps may not realize what comparatively sterile and limited documents we've got; and I don't want our...book on the subject to be written by a dirty great committee! So I will tread cautiously.' A few months later, he told Bennett: 'Chadwick and I have not sold our souls to the Institute of Classical Studies in any way, or shown them any unpublished tablets.'

He and his idea were becoming public property, whether he liked it or not. Before the beginning of the seminar, Ventris had been made an honorary research associate at University College; now the University of Uppsala (the oldest university in northern Europe) conferred an honorary doctorate on him at the age of 31; the following year, he would receive an OBE from the Queen. There were also articles about him and Linear B in *Scientific American*, *Time* magazine, the *New York Times*, and many other lesser magazines and newspapers. The *Time* interview went well, Ventris told Chadwick, but there was less comprehension from the science correspondent of the *New York Times*: 'as his own field was wasps, some of the talk about ideograms etc. was a bit difficult. "Was Mycenia a big country" etc...'. Another *New York Times* article published at this time alleged, rather ludicrously, a link between certain signs at Stonehenge and 'the recently decoded Minoan syllabary'. It reported that 'At a working height of four feet from the ground, the architect left behind his mark, the axes and the dagger sign.' Someone – maybe Ventris himself – has written wittily in the margin of the copy of the article preserved in Ventris's papers: 'How clever of Tessa to reach that high!' (Tessa Ventris was then an eight-year-old.)

In June, Ventris decided that the time was ripe to get started on the big joint book for scholars that he had been discussing with Chadwick since the previous year. 'I don't much want to write the "popular decipherment" kind of book, though a section of it must deal with methods', he told him in a letter from Athens. Several publishers were interested; Ventris and Chadwick soon settled on Cambridge University Press, as recommended by Chadwick.

Documents in Mycenaean Greek, as the book was finally titled, is something of a bible of Linear B studies, consisting of five introductory chapters on the decipherment itself and what it has revealed about the Mycenaean writing system, language, personal names and society, followed by the detailed interpretation of 300 Linear B tablets grouped into chapters such as 'Livestock and agricultural produce' and 'Textiles, vessels and furniture', and an extensive glossary of Mycenaean words. There is also a long foreword by Wace, the excavator of Mycenae and professor of classical archaeology at Cambridge who had been the chief victim in the 1920s of Sir Arthur Evans's Minoan 'imperialism' and was therefore delighted by the evidence of the tablets.

Ventris decided on the original scheme of the book, then he and Chadwick divided between them the writing of particular chapters. Drafts of these were exchanged and criticized by each other. Sometimes this led to material being completely scrapped, but on the whole the drafts became the framework onto which bits were then fitted by the other writer. 'It's impossible to read the book now and say "That is Ventris and that is Chadwick",' remarked Chadwick in the 1980s in *Michael Ventris Remembered*, after producing his second edition of *Documents* in 1973. 'There are certain people' – he was thinking of Palmer among others – 'who have since said that everything that's right in the book is Ventris's and everything that's wrong is mine, but I'm afraid that isn't quite true!' He and Ventris did have some friendly disagreements, and very occasionally these survive in printed form in the footnotes of *Documents* – but the vast majority of the interpretations were jointly agreed, even if more of the book was written by Ventris than by Chadwick.

For most of that summer of 1954 Ventris was in Greece, and he returned there again the following summer. In the one-year interval between his visits, *Documents in Mycenaean Greek* was swiftly written, incorporating the very latest tablets from Crete, Pylos and Mycenae, which Ventris translated almost as they came out of the ground, to the excitement of the Greek workmen in the trenches. The Mycenae tablets were especially interesting because they included a list of spices such as cumin, fennel, sesame, coriander and mint, and real seeds were also found (though unfortunately they did not live up to hopes that the botanists would match plants and Linear B names). Bennett and Wace offered all possible assistance, but there was some attempt at secrecy from Blegen, which crumbled in the face of Ventris's charm and by now unavoidable fame.

Officially, during both those summers he had gone to Greece as an architect, i.e. a draughtsman-surveyor, for a new British excavation directed by a friend, Sinclair Hood, at the rather remote little harbour of Emborio near the southern tip of Chios, one of the Greek islands off the coast of Turkey. The site had been settled during Minoan times in the early Bronze Age, abandoned at the end of the Bronze Age, and then reoccupied by Greeks in early classical times despite the rugged mountain terrain around the harbour. It was Ventris's task, helped by his wife some of the time, to map the structures from various periods that the excavators and he discovered. Although there were no tablet finds, here was a nearly ideal, not to say idyllic way to combine his two key interests: architecture and decipherment.

It is revealing to compare two verbal snapshots of Ventris at Emborio. Dilys Powell, the writer and Hellenophile, was there as a relatively casual visitor. She saw 'a reserved young man with dark hair and serious refined features', who with his wife formed an 'industrious pair' regularly to be seen 'setting off with their notebooks in the long shadows of early morning or the stunning heat of afternoon towards the foundations of an archaic temple high in a hollow of the hills', as she wrote in *The Villa Ariadne* in the 1970s.

John Boardman, one of the expedition's archaeologists (later professor of classical archaeology at Oxford), remembered vividly almost fifty years later someone who was 'quiet, witty, generous, not at all "imposing"

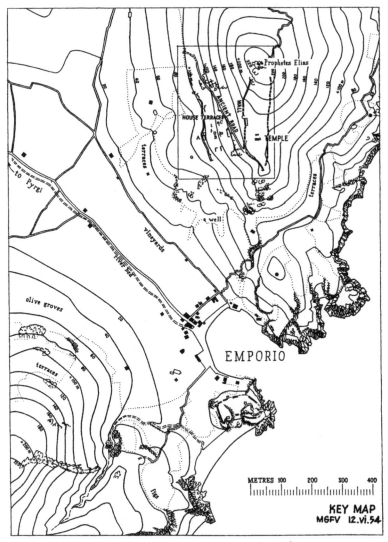

A site map of Emporio (or Emborio), Chios, drawn by Ventris, 1954.

despite his achievement with Linear B, nor at all scholarly in the usual way'. But it was Ventris's ability to improvise that struck Boardman most. 'Drawing walls in the excavation trenches he would rely, in the drawing of stones, more on what he knew to be the length of his own foot than on tedious measuring with a tape; he threatened to paint his wife in 50 cm stripes so that she could serve as a mobile sighting pole; he devised various impromptu aids for the excavator such as a simple way of determining circumference from sherds. There seemed a sort of instinctive method in everything that he did which went beyond the commonplace – he found a bracelet dropped by my wife in a grassy field which we had given up for lost – and he deduced areas to search and what to observe. He was intrepid too: while scuba-diving he speared an eel which we ate. It seemed not at all surprising that such a man could have both the patience and the vision to achieve the decipherment, since it required

Michael, Lois and Tessa Ventris on holiday.

both, to a high degree. He seemed interested in everything and challenged to understand everything.... He was really not a humanities intellectual at all.'

In fact diving became quite a passion with Ventris. It took him a week of tracking the eel to its lair off the coast before he finally got it. (Sadly it tasted like fishy 'cotton wool', according to Sinclair Hood's future wife Rachel.) A letter written to his wife in early August, after she left for home to look after the children, is decorated with a charming sketch of himself in goggles, snorkel and flippers, swimming backwards and playing 'follow my leader' with some small fish. And he wrote to Chadwick: 'I have a daily encounter with a really large green fish in a hole under the rocks, but he's outwitted me so far and is getting warier every day.'

Then he returned to the world of classical linguistic scholarship. In late August, no doubt sporting a superb tan, he addressed the 2nd International Classical Congress in Copenhagen, one of his favourite cities. When he showed his best exhibit, the slide of the 'tripods' tablet P641, the whole of the large audience burst into applause before he had said a word (as reported to Chadwick – but not by the reticent Ventris). However he cautioned the audience that although many key scholars now agreed that the Linear B language was Greek, 'ten people can be just as wrong as one'. Chadwick, to his great disappointment, could not attend the conference because his fare was not paid and he did not feel able to accept Ventris's offer to pay it himself.

Offers to join the academic world (although he had not even attended a university) were now his for the asking. But Ventris spurned them all. In November 1954, for instance, he was invited to give the Waynflete lectures at Oxford in 1955–56, following Lewis Namier, Max Born, Steven Runciman and other very distinguished figures. The hope was that he would bring the significance of the decipherment to a wider audience 'in a way likely to cut across faculty boundaries'. He replied significantly: 'Though it is unfashionable to confess it, I am chiefly interested in the more esoteric technicalities of the subject, in the details of writing systems and language structure. There are already ample signs of readiness among archaeologists, historians and Homeric scholars to explore the wider implications of the tenuous clues which Chadwick and I hope to have provided, and I feel they are better qualified to do this than I am.' His priority, he said, must be to complete *Documents in Mycenaean Greek*. He also remarked that since he was 'by profession an architect', he did not want to commit himself to Mycenaean studies too far into the future.

The writing of the big book was now entering its most intense phase, with Ventris and Chadwick in constant and lengthy communication by letter, and very occasional meetings between them. Their discussion was almost exclusively technical, at a level requiring a deep knowledge of Greek, so it is impenetrable to all but specialists. Many details they debated remain unresolved to this day. However there are a few points that are more generally accessible and that illustrate the problems of decipherment mentioned earlier. We shall look at only two.

The phrase *tiripo eme pode owowe* in the 'tripods' tablet illustrated on page 119 was translated by Ventris and Chadwick as 'tripod cauldron with a single handle on one foot'. But this does not match the pictogram accompanying the phrase, 🝂, which definitely shows a tripod cauldron with two handles. The meanings in Greek of the three words, *eme* ('one' in the dative case), *pode* ('foot' in the dative case) and *owowe* ('one-handled'), are not really in dispute, since they are supported by clear analogies in the rest of the 'tripods' tablet and in some other tablets. The difficulty is how to combine the words plausibly. Since, judging from the pictogram, the top of the tripod could not be one-handled, the single handle could only be on the foot of the tripod; Ventris and Chadwick showed a drawing of an excavated Mycenaean 'incense burner' in support of their contention:

However this interpretation was obviously open to criticism, so in the second edition of *Documents* published long after Ventris's death, Chadwick offered a new one: that the tripod cauldron has only one handle *and* only one foot (the other two must have been broken off or burnt off) – in other words, *owowe* and *eme pode* are taken separately, no longer together. So why then does the pictogram show a cauldron with two handles and three feet? In response, Chadwick suggested that the 'the effort of depicting recognizably a tripod cauldron with two of its feet missing would be beyond the artistic powers of the scribe', and that the sign is actually a 'stereotype', which does not show the missing feet (or the missing handle). Supporting this stereotype notion, the American classicist Tom Palaima (a student of Bennett) observed: 'I was not troubled when I saw a bare-headed man in jeans and a T-shirt come out of a men's room in a restaurant in south-west Turkey that was identified on its door by a pictogram of a tall thin man in a conservative Cary Grant suit wearing a stetson hat and smoking a pipe. The distinctive feature of a tripod is its three feet, even if two happen to be damaged or missing in a particular instance.' Agreed, but still the explanation seems a little lame. On the very same tablet, the scribe plainly had no difficulty in representing goblets with four, three and no handles. There seems no compelling reason why a tripod cauldron should be depicted stereotypically, but a goblet should look realistic.

The second problem is in some ways easier to grasp. Another Pylos tablet, very carelessly written and therefore hard to read, nevertheless clearly contains the names of gods and goddesses and mentions the bringing of gold bowls and people to a shrine. For instance, one line reads: 'To Posidaeia: one gold bowl, one woman'; another: 'To Zeus: one gold bowl, one man'. The tablet's introductory line contains the word *po-re-na*, which appears to define the nature of all this sacrificial activity, but its meaning here is not clear, though other words definitely say that some of the gifts were 'carried' to the shrine, while other gifts were 'led'. The first edition of *Documents* contained a faint hint that human sacrifice was involved, but by the time of the second edition, human sacrifice was accepted, at least by Chadwick, as a likely explanation – despite the revulsion of many scholars – partly because archaeological evidence had been discovered suggesting that the Mycenaeans may have sacrificed human beings. (More evidence has appeared since 1973.) As he wrote in *The Mycenaean World* in 1976, 'though the Greeks of the classical age disapproved of the practice, they were familiar with it from Homer, and it forms an essential element in the plot of many tragedies.' Possibly the Pylos victims were hastily sacrificed to avert the fall of the city, just before its end, which might account for the scribbled poverty of the signs. But having said this, less lurid interpretations are possible; and the fact remains that there are many disputed meanings in this tablet.

The typing of *Documents in Mycenaean Greek* was done by Ventris, partly on a Varityper at University College London. It was a complex and demanding job, made harder by this technology – at least in comparison to an electronic word processor. 'I wish I could pay God to finish it', Ventris wearily joked to the Greek scholar Eric Handley who occupied the office next door. But by the time he left for Greece in the summer of 1955, the labour was done. In July, Chadwick handed over the complete manuscript to Cambridge University Press, and informed Ventris in Greece with a postcard written in Linear B.

By the time he returned to England, it appears that Ventris was beginning to lose interest in the new subject he had launched. His letters to Chadwick and Bennett tail off. He did continue to attend the meetings of the London seminar, and he did agree to take part in an inaugural International Colloquium of 'Mycenologists' (a new word in the scholarly lexicon) scheduled for April 1956, which was to be held near Paris at the Centre National de la Recherche Scientifique (CNRS), organized by two scholars from a country that had hitherto played remarkably little part in the decipherment. Yet one senses that Ventris's heart was not in the meeting.

He complained to Chadwick about scholars such as Palmer 'frittering our whole energy away in discussion'. 'The whole Paris thing is *rather* a bore, but evidently we must prepare something for it. I have the feeling that 95% of our time gets used up on administration rather than creative work, but I suppose that's the penalty for the start we have on the others.' By early December, while Palmer was 'showering...rather magisterial missives' on the organizers of the London seminar, Ventris got back to the Varityper to produce an index of Mycenaean vocabulary for the French meeting. 'It's quite a job, as I am having to check through about six lists and books simultaneously'. Finally, in what appears to have been his very last letter to Chadwick, written just before Christmas, he informed his collaborator: 'I seem to have lined myself up a year's *architectural* research job beginning mid-January. This won't affect Paris, which I shall attend; nor, I hope, will it cut down the speed I can get proof-reading of the book done. But it means I shan't be able to devote time to any other major commitments. Once the two present pieces of typing are done, there's not much for me to do anyway except argue with Palmer, and that comes better from you.'

Once again, as in 1948 when he abruptly cut off from Sir John Myres's publication of *Scripta Minoa*, Ventris's inner conflict had surfaced disruptively. In the final year of his life, it would become even more acute.

8

Triumph and Tragedy

'The peculiarities of [my] mind and personality have turned on me and made me deeply doubt the value both of my vaunted intelligence and to a large extent that of life itself.'

Michael Ventris in a letter to an architect, August 1956

The 'architectural research job' that Ventris had taken on at the beginning of 1956 was a project of considerable prestige. He was to be the very first research fellow appointed by a distinguished board of architects at the behest of the *Architects' Journal* (*AJ*), the leading British publication for the profession, with a brief to conduct research 'which will be of direct benefit to the architect in practice'. The award was worth £1000 for one year, to be paid by the journal's publishers, the Architectural Press. Ventris chose to study 'Information for the architect: what does he need and where will it come from' – a subject which had clear resonance with his decipherment of Linear B.

From the point of view of the early 21st century, when we are inundated with instantaneously available information of all kinds, it is not easy to imagine the situation for British architects in the mid-1950s, as the post-war economy began to boom. For a start, there were almost no books on architectural design, explaining how to design a school, a hospital or a factory; the typical architects' design office did not even have a bookshelf. Manufacturers' product samples were of course available, and were becoming more sophisticated, but they were printed in such a wide

Ventris, architect and decipherer.

range of sizes that filing them for easy reference in a busy office was a major headache, if this was done at all. There was almost no organized analysis and assessment of products for the benefit of consumers (the Consumers' Association and its magazine *Which?* were yet to come). As for government and university research on new materials and building techniques, although this was rapidly increasing in amount and scope, the results were not filtering through to architects effectively. 'One of the misfortunes of architectural practice in this country is the way in which teaching, research and practice are largely kept separate and apart', an *AJ* editorial bemoaned.

Most professionals involved in the construction of buildings knew that a serious problem was looming. Architects were in an especially weak position. 'A profession of generalists was about to be blown away by an explosion of social, technical and legal knowledge, all in the hands of specialists of innumerable types not particularly anxious in any way to help a profession seen as dilettantes concerned with pretty drawings and high fees but which was being handed by government massive problems to solve, for which as a whole it was ill equipped.' This is from Dargan Bullivant, Ventris's former colleague at the Ministry of Education in 1949–50, who took up Ventris's research fellowship after his death. Or to put the problem in Ventris's own inimitable words: 'Even in offices with lavish information services it may be difficult to get architects to use them, owing to their natural "information resistance" – the feeling that it is easier to produce a design decision sitting at the drawing board, from memory, common sense and rule of thumb, than to have to take a walk each time and check on the latest state of knowledge.'

In February, Ventris presented a truly formidable, not to say forbidding analysis of his job to the research board for its approval. His report is reminiscent of the questionnaire he sent out to Minoan script scholars in late 1949, which led to the *Mid-Century Report* of 1950. Having methodically set out his 'terms of reference' and the diverse ways he proposed to explore them, he listed eight 'reasons for complaint' and their possible remedies: a slightly ambiguous form of words since 'complaint' could mean both complaint *by* architects and complaint *against* architects, but which was inevitably a recognition of the fundamentally negative nature of the task ahead of him. Reason 1 was: 'The architect does not realize he needs information on a particular problem/does not bother to get it/is not qualified to use it intelligently.' (Ventris commented realistically: 'This is not likely to be elicited from the architects themselves.') Reason 8, the most interesting, was: 'The architect is presented with inconclusive or contradictory information on problems of building technique, and no independent authority is prepared to give guidance on the relative merits of alternative products and systems.' Under 'possible remedies' for the latter situation, Ventris listed: 'More fundamental research by the bodies best suited to undertake it./ Fuller publication of research already done./ More explicit indications of specific products to which theoretical conclusions may be taken to apply./ A wider application of official seals of approval to products and systems./ Some way of getting around the law of libel to provide consumer assessments of products./ More and better "synthetic" books and articles covering particular forms of building technique./ More detailed and critical evaluation of technical details of buildings, published in the press, including a study of how they wear.' However he recognized, summing up, that his remedies were not 'necessarily...feasible ones'.

It was a far-sighted programme – but as Ventris must have known, even before he subjected selected architects' offices during the first half of 1956 to 'a sort of urbane "third degree"' (in the words of the *AJ*, after his death), much of the programme was also far from being feasible under contemporary conditions. Now, he was not manipulating Linear B signs in his mind and in Work Notes, or 'group working' with a few like-minded students at the AA, but instead dealing with the ingrained habits of hundreds of professional architects, not to mention their contractors and suppliers. Half a century later, we can admire his prescient thoughts on automation in 'an Information Centre of the future'. ('One might ring up the information centre to ask for any information, say, on *aluminium schools* in Australia; the information officer would operate a keyboard with the UDC numbers for *aluminium, school* and *Australia*; the microcards comprising the complete information of the centre would be sorted for those sharing these codings; the selected cards would have their articles transmitted electronically to a view or printer at the subscriber's

Scholars at the Mycenaean conference in Gif, France, 1956. Chadwick, with dark hair and glasses, second row left of centre; Ventris and Bennett, back row, third and second from right.

desk.') But in 1956, to most working architects, this vision would have seemed merely far-fetched.

At the end of March, he took a break from interviewing: first, to ski in Switzerland, then to visit the long-planned Mycenaean colloquium in France. 'He arrived bronzed and looking very fit, whereas the rest of us were pale after the winter', Chadwick recalled. There were eight French scholars participating, and eleven foreigners, all staying in a chateau at Gif just outside Paris. Ventris, of course, was the centre of attention, not only because of what he had done but also because of his exceptional linguistic abilities: he spoke to the French in fluent French, the Swiss in Swiss German, and the Greek delegate in Greek. And his modesty and sense of humour set the tone of the meeting. 'Now at the first sign of a quarrel, we have only to appeal to the *esprit de Gif*,' wrote Chadwick in *The Decipherment of Linear B*.

In the evenings, rather than providing dinner, the organizers gave the delegates money to go into Paris and entertain themselves. Mostly, Ventris, Chadwick and Bennett would spend the time together chatting pleasantly about things other than Linear B; it was really the first time any of them had done this in four years of intensive scholarly correspondence. However, one evening, Ventris and Bennett went off to a Paris nightclub without Chadwick. The following morning at breakfast, Professor Chantraine, the seniormost figure among the organizers, politely asked Ventris where he had been the previous evening. 'Michael told him,' recalled Chadwick in *Michael Ventris Remembered*. 'Chantraine looked at him and asked him who had told him to go *there*. Michael looked most embarrassed and said, "As a matter of fact, it was Madame Chantraine!"'

Bennett had fond memories of these days spent with Ventris. But he was most taken aback when Michael told him quite directly that he himself saw no future in Linear B. And he clearly meant what he said. Apart from reading the proofs of *Documents in Mycenaean Greek*, he would take no further part in Mycenaean studies before he died. As already remarked (in the Introduction), it was the *puzzle* of Linear B that had truly appealed to him, not what could be learnt from the tablets – and once the puzzle was solved, he lost interest, as he hinted in a talk about the Gif meeting broadcast on the BBC's European Service on 1 May. (Typically, though, he offered to do versions of it in many other European languages.)

During May, he was elected by a substantial vote to the council of the Architectural Association. Yet he was becoming very disenchanted with his work for the research fellowship, the first part of which he submitted to the *AJ* board in June. Very likely, his recent series of contacts with working architects had served to remind him, forcibly, of the fact that he was doing no design work of his own, and that he had not become a member of an architectural firm, unlike many of his friends from student days at the AA. The closest of them, Oliver Cox, had somewhat lost touch with Ventris during the heyday of the decipherment, being very busy with design work and having also got married in 1953. But he was aware that his gifted friend was constantly depressed that spring and summer. The old struggle with the creative part of design work ('sharawaggi') was again at the forefront of Ventris's mind. 'I was very conscious of his worries and his frustration that every time he got an architectural job he was pushed towards his capacity as an analyst.... He was desperately frustrated by the fact that he couldn't get involved in a design team doing the sort of work he wanted to do. It was very distressing to him. His research work on information for architects in his last year was, I think, a mistake, because it pushed him further in that direction and made people realize how brilliant he was at sorting papers out.' On what would be the last occasion the two friends would talk, in a car on the way back home from the AA, Cox strongly advised Ventris to extract himself from the fellowship. At the same time, Ventris had a heart-to-heart talk about the problem with William Allen, a sympathetic member of the *AJ*'s research board who was superintending architect at the government's Building Research Station.

So far as is known, Ventris never discussed these anxieties with his wife Lois. He had always tended to bottle up his deepest concerns, and there were many areas of his life in which Lois had little interest. She was in no sense an intellectual and undoubtedly resented his long love affair with Linear B, and she had never liked the shy, scholarly Chadwick, whom she thought (unfairly) had attached himself to Michael for career reasons. Even with regard to architecture, their chief shared interest, Lois had none of her husband's capacity for analysis. Although their house at 19 North End is often described as a joint design by both the Ventrises, it is obvious from the drawings that almost all the real thinking and execution was done by Michael alone. By 1956, after fourteen years of marriage, the Ventrises had drifted quite far apart. A friend from the Ministry of

Education, Edward Samuel – the same friend who used to help Ventris with decipherment in his lunchbreaks – took several enjoyable holidays with the Ventrises in the 1950s (including a most uncomfortable night spent *à trois* in a heavily dewed tent pitched in the garden of Ben Nicholson and Barbara Hepworth at St Ives). One day, Lois told him candidly that the reason he was invited along was because otherwise she and Michael would simply run out of conversation.

The children remained a bond between them of course, but not a very strong one. The Ventrises could afford to leave their children in the care of others, and, as was the custom among their set in the 1950s, they often chose to do so. Moreover, like many intellectually inclined people, Michael was ambivalent about parenthood; the very design of 19 North End reflects this, with its deliberate separation of the children's rooms on the ground floor from those of the parents upstairs. (A *Country Life* article on the house is entitled 'Keeping the children under'.) As Nikki Ventris admitted to the authors of *Michael Ventris Remembered* in a letter, written just two days before his own death from a heart attack in 1983 at the age of 40: 'My father was a private person and shared few of his concerns with us. In fact he seemed rather remote and very absorbed in his work to the exclusion of family life. That is not to say that he was incapable of enjoying himself: on occasion he took his part in family outings and games with obvious pleasure and we were always pleased to have his company.... I did not know my father at all well, and it was only at and after his death that I realized how much I had missed in not getting to know him better.'

Perhaps this psychological background explains, if only a little, the extraordinary, shocking, abject, private letter, handwritten in his usual immaculate, print-like script, that Ventris now wrote to the editor of the *Architects' Journal*:

I have had a couple of weeks abroad, and had a chance to get into perspective the hash that I've been making of your Fellowship; I've come to the conclusion that it's quite unrealistic for me to pretend to you or to myself that I'm going to be able to finish off the work in the way that it should be done. I'm afraid I must ask you again, as I have done since April, to devise some formula, however humiliating to myself, for relieving me of the second part of the task.

I am mortally ashamed of the waste of time and energy that this false start means for those who have been associated with the Fellowship. It would be easy to say that the 'information' subject was a dangerous research subject, and that it was risky to pick on me to do it; but the fault lies in me, and I know how worthwhile the job would be if one could do it well. The peculiarities of mind and personality which seemed to make me suited for the Fellowship have turned on me and made me deeply doubt the value of both my vaunted intelligence and to a large extent that of life itself. I've had to turn for professional advice to help me sort out my life and meanwhile I feel it's quite presumptuous to set myself up to attack anyone else's problems, either on the high level demanded by the Board or with the glibness required by the *Journal*.

The money I've so far received from you on account will have to be paid back apart from any value that you may put on the work I have already turned in: perhaps that can stand as some sort of contribution, though I know only too well how cold and dull it all is. As for explaining to *AJ* readers why the second half of the programme has flopped, you'd be justified in writing me off in a way that will make it difficult to hold up my head in the ranks of architects again, and bring pain to my family. All I can ask you is to temper your justifiable anger with a little compassion.

Yours,
Michael Ventris

The letter is dated 22 August 1956. Scarcely two weeks after he wrote it, aged only 34, Ventris was dead. Near midnight on 5 September he left 19 North End alone, and just before 1 a.m., for unknown reasons (according to his wife), he was driving on the Barnet bypass near Hatfield, north of London, when his car collided at high speed with a lorry parked in a lay-by; and he was killed instantly. The verdict of the jury at the coroner's inquest was 'accidental death'.

Perhaps the lorry was not showing its lights, as was suggested at the inquest (and denied by the lorry driver). Perhaps Ventris's mind became distracted by his evident worries at the wrong moment (he was not a good driver, as he had not been a confident pilot). Perhaps he had a heart attack (as his son Nikki would). Perhaps, even, he was affected by defective night vision, as implied by his pilot father-in-law at the inquest (though there is no evidence of his suffering from this condition in his wartime letters to his wife – otherwise how could he have been a superb navigator?). Perhaps it was suicide (as some of his friends have wondered), like the death of his mother. Perhaps, perhaps, perhaps....

As Oliver Cox told Lois Ventris just before her death in 1987, there is small point in speculating. No one will ever know for certain what happened that night. Like so many other facets of Michael Ventris, his death, too, was unconventional and mysterious.

The obituaries dwelt, without any hyperbole, on his youth, his good humour, his perfectionism, his 'genius', and above all his understatement and modesty. 'Those who knew Michael Ventris at the "AA" will remember his kindness, sincerity and sense of fun. Great modesty hid his brilliant powers,' said the *Architectural Association Journal*. Patrick Hunter, his former teacher at Stowe, remembered Michael's lecture at the school after the decipherment: 'a model of lucidity, spiced with much entertainment, the whole delivered with an enviable degree of objectivity. He was so obviously unspoiled by the fame which in a world wider than that of specialists and scholars he had surely won, so loth to make claims for himself and so ready to acknowledge the work of others.' John Chadwick wrote in *The Times*: 'It was typical of him that he sought no honours, and preferred not to speak of those he received. He was always modest and unassuming, and his charm and wit made him the most agreeable of companions. Nothing was too much trouble for him, and he gave generously of his time and services. Perhaps only those who knew him will fully understand the tragedy of his untimely death.' While a French scholar, Professor Dumézil, who had known him only at Gif, commented simply and truly: 'Devant les siècles son oeuvre est faite.'*

On Ventris's plain gravestone in the village of Welford in Northamptonshire, where his mother's family came from, only these words are written:

MICHAEL VENTRIS

WHO FIRST READ THE

MINOAN LINEAR B

SCRIPT AS GREEK

1922–1956

This much, at least, will forever be known about a unique Englishman.

---

* 'In the centuries to come his reputation is made.'

Postscript

'The most interesting fact about his work is that it forced [Michael Ventris] to propose a solution contrary to his own preconceptions.'
John Chadwick, 1975

Within months of his tragic death, those who had known Michael Ventris, and other admirers who had not, got together to found a memorial scholarship in his name. Under the joint umbrella of the Architectural Association and the Institute of Classical Studies in London, the scholarship was to be given to young architects and young scholars in Mycenaean Greek studies on the threshold of promising careers, with the award alternating between Ventris's two fields. Founded in 1957, the scholarship gradually established itself and has been given to students annually ever since.

Documents in Mycenaean Greek was published in the autumn of 1956, sadly too late for one of its authors. There were many reviews, both in the specialist journals and in the national press, such was the interest generated by the decipherment and by the personality of Ventris himself. Tom Webster, the moving spirit behind the London seminar, wrote in *Antiquity*: 'Two impressions strike the reader at once. First the immense amount of scholarship of different kinds, linguistic, archaeological and historical, that has gone into it in an extraordinarily short time, since only three years separate the publication of the original article in the *Journal of Hellenic Studies* from the publication of this book. This period included a great deal of intensive work on the tablets in many different countries, and the authors have taken this into account and have dealt very justly and courteously with all their fellow-workers. The second impression is the beauty and clarity of the book production, which is up to the highest standards of the Cambridge Press.' Later in the review, Webster remarked: 'Thus the foundations are soundly laid for future work. They are sound because the authors are cautious; but because they are foundations laid by a cunning architect, they will determine to a large degree the shape of the building.' And he concluded: 'Enough has been said to show that this book opens a new world, and it is heartbreaking that the ingenuity, wisdom and sanity of Michael Ventris can no longer guide us in its exploration.'

But other scholars were by no means so generous. Palmer from Oxford University, while signally saluting Ventris and the decipherment, was at pains to distance his solo achievement from his joint work with Chadwick. 'One must regretfully acknowledge that there is much in the second half of *Documents* which is wholly unacceptable and even palpably absurd.'

Beattie from Edinburgh University (last heard of at the celebrated June 1953 lecture by Ventris), went much further. Nicknamed 'Linear Beattie' by his friends, he had founded in Scotland what came to be mockingly called an 'anti-decipherment seminar'. He had been sceptical about the decipherment right from the start, claiming in a 1952 letter to Chadwick, whom Beattie had taught at Cambridge, that he had tried the Greek solution some years previously and had found the evidence for it insufficient. But his first major published attack appeared (in the *Journal of Hellenic Studies*) only in 1956, which unfortunately for Beattie coincided with the very month of Ventris's death. Thereafter, his accusations became ferocious and extremely libellous, although he took the precaution of accusing only Ventris of malfeasance and not Chadwick. In a so-called *Plain Guide* to the decipherment, Beattie openly stated that

Ventris had 'somehow' obtained a drawing of the famous 'tripods' tablet from Pylos, not from Blegen in May 1953, but in early June 1952, immediately after its excavation, and had written Work Note 20 in the full, but private knowledge of this tablet: in other words, Ventris had 'fixed' the decipherment in advance. When Blegen subsequently stated the facts of P641's excavation, showing that Ventris's foreknowledge of the tablet was physically impossible, Beattie publicly withdrew his allegation – but substituted another even more fantastic: that a similar tablet had been communicated to Ventris at an even earlier stage in the decipherment. This he accompanied with some personal comments on Ventris which would be breathtakingly malicious were they not so comically off the mark, like some bathetic imitation of an Agatha Christie murder mystery. ('Although the contents of all the Work Notes were guarded from the public eye by the author during his life and are kept unpublished by his supporters in England since his death, a complete set has recently come into the possession of Edinburgh University Library' – and much more in the same vein.) Beattie's *odium scholasticum* against the amateur Ventris broke all sane bounds and proved only that envy is corrosive, perhaps especially in the intellectual world.

What is the point in raking over the embers of this scholarly animosity many decades after all but a tiny handful of incorrigible scholars has accepted the decipherment as valid? Chiefly because Beattie scored one authentic hit that still reverberates today, if allowance is made for its sarcastic ring. 'We may safely discount any pretence that the decipherment is safeguarded by sound cryptographic method or that it is strictly controlled by the grid. The truth is that the grid was inadequate at the outset to control the first experimental identifications [i.e. the substitutions that produced the names of Cretan towns like Amnisos] and that it was quickly modified to accommodate an increasing number of conjectures.'

As this account has shown, the decipherment was indeed *not* a triumph of logical deduction. It was emphatically not like a mathematical proof. In a well-known book on cryptography, *The Codebreakers* by David Kahn, the Linear B decipherment is said to 'shine with a clean Euclidean beauty. In it, man thinks more purely rationally, depending less upon external information and more upon logical manipulation of the data to derive new conclusions, than perhaps anywhere else in the humanities.' But this is nonsense – comforting though such an ideal may be to those who seek at least a few refuges of pure rationality outside the 'hard' sciences. In reality, the decipherment is something much more fascinating. Perhaps Chadwick encapsulated Ventris's true approach the most succinctly when he wrote (not in the over-rationalized *Decipherment of Linear B* but in a much later piece): 'The most interesting fact about his work is that it forced him to propose a solution contrary to his own preconceptions.'

While it is right, and vital to vigorous intellectual life and scholarly activity, that we try to understand what arguments led Ventris to his key conclusion, and test their logical validity, the unavoidable fact is that the decipherment was an inextricable combination of intuition and logic, with the second controlling the (not always reliable) leaps of the first. This is why Ventris was a genius – and not a Beattie, or even a Chadwick or a Bennett.

And we can go further, and say that the same is true of all great scientists. The myth that science proceeds only by the 'scientific method' – in which irrefutable knowledge of the physical world accumulates from the gradual accretion of experimental observations – dies hard, but die it should. One hesitates to quote Einstein here, given his iconic reputation as a rationalist, but he knew very well that science works through many kinds of mental activity. Meditating on the mystery of how Kepler discovered that the planets had orbits that were ellipses (a geometrical form that was itself a discovery of the ancient Greek geometers), Einstein wrote: 'It seems that the human mind has first to construct forms, independently, before we can find them in things. Kepler's marvellous achievement is a particularly fine example of the fact that knowledge cannot spring from experience alone but only from a comparison of the inventions of the intellect with the facts of observation.' Ventris, one feels, would have entirely agreed with this. *Inventing* was what he was doing when he dreamt up the idea that Kober's 'triplets' might contain the names of real Minoan towns. His painstaking comparison of his hypothesis with the actual sign groups fitted the facts. His hypothesis about Etruscan names in the tablets did not – and as a 'scientist' he abandoned it, albeit very reluctantly.

As for what the humanities – archaeologists, historians, literary scholars and others – have learnt from the decipherment since Ventris's death, the answer is, honestly speaking, a little disappointing, set beside the artistic treasures and legends of Troy, Mycenae and Knossos. A 'new world' may have opened up for Greek specialists like Webster, but its boundaries are strictly circumscribed. No great battles, great thoughts or great poetry. The rate of discovery of tablets has slowed dramatically since Ventris's time, though there have been a few minor excitements, such as a clay tablet found at Pylos in 1957 with a list of men and goats on one side and a drawing of a labyrinth on the other – presumably a doodle by an idle scribe, since the drawing has nothing to do with the list:

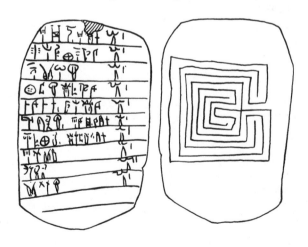

There has turned out to be nothing of literary value in Linear B: the tablets merely record prosaic details of palace administration – lists of names and their trades and lists of goods – though careful detective work on them has shed light on Mycenaean society as a whole, such as the possibility of human sacrifice mentioned in chapter 7. Here too, Ventris's hunch about the future of Linear B studies, expressed to a surprised Bennett at the Gif meeting, has proved correct.

In that last BBC broadcast, in May 1956, Ventris concluded: 'There are further questions still, which Wace is fond of asking, but to which we may never be able to find an answer. The first of these is: "Did epic poetry of the school of Homer already exist in Mycenaean times, and was it perhaps already committed to writing?" The second is "Was knowledge of writing really lost suddenly in about 1200 B.C. [with the fall of Pylos], and was there really a period of about 400 years when the Greeks were quite illiterate, until the introduction of the Greek alphabet that we know?"' Fifty years after Ventris's ground-breaking decipherment, the answers to these interesting and significant questions still elude us.

Further Reading
Index
Picture Credits

Further Reading

As this book is not written primarily for scholars, I have not footnoted my sources, which are both published and unpublished. This note does not attempt to list all of them, because it is intended as a guide for those who want to explore various aspects of Michael Ventris and his work – his personal life; the decipherment of Linear B; the Minoan and Mycenaean world; and Ventris as an architect – without going into scholarly depth. Rather than listing further reading according to each chapter of the book, I have therefore divided the note into four sections according to the above categories. (Place of publication of books is the United Kingdom unless otherwise mentioned.)

Ventris's life

The best source is the booklet, *Michael Ventris Remembered*, published by Stowe School in 1984, by Simon Tetlow, Ben Harris, David Roques and A. G. Meredith, with a foreword by John Chadwick. This was based on interviews done by three boys then at the school (Tetlow, Harris and Roques), which were ably edited by a master (Meredith). It gives a broad-ranging and lively portrait of Ventris, without being wholly reliable.

Chapter 1 of John Chadwick's *The Decipherment of Linear B* is a brief, somewhat formal sketch of Ventris's life. There is an even briefer recollection of Ventris by Ian Martin in 'Some memories of the early "Minoan Linear B Seminars"', in the 44th Annual Report of the Institute of Classical Studies for 1996–97. Patrick Hunter wrote a substantial obituary in the Stowe school magazine, *The Stoic*, in March 1957. Other obituaries are in the Ventris Papers at the Institute of Classical Studies.

Regarding Ventris's early life up to his marriage, the Stowe archives have a number of letters written by Ventris's parents and by himself to the staff; copies of Dorothea Ventris's letters to Marcel Breuer are in the Ventris Papers; his letters to Naum Gabo and Ben Nicholson are in the Tate Gallery archives. An enjoyable account of Hampstead in the 1930s is *View from the Long Chair*, a memoir by Jack Pritchard (1984), with a long introduction by Fiona MacCarthy. For a detailed description of the building of Highpoint, see *Lubetkin: Architecture and the Tradition of Progress*, by John Allan (1992). An excellent account of Stowe in the 1930s is *Roxburgh of Stowe*, by Noel Annan (1965).

On the war years, there are numerous personal letters written by Ventris to his wife, and his most interesting diary for 1945–46, in the Ventris Papers. *The Bomber Command War Diaries: An Operational Reference Book, 1939–45* by Martin Middlebrook and Chris Everitt (1985) describes the missions flown by 76 Squadron.

The notes, drawings, cartoons and letters arising from Ventris's visit to Stockholm with Oliver Cox and Graeme Shankland in 1947, are in the Ventris Papers. So too is the spring-backed design book kept by Ventris in the late 1940s.

Prudence Smith's account of Ventris's BBC broadcast in 1952 appears in her memoirs, *The Morning Light: A South African Childhood Revealed* (Cape Town, 2000).

On his life after the decipherment, there are some letters to his wife written from Greece in the Ventris Papers, which also contain his letter rejecting the offer of the Waynflete lectures at Oxford University. His 'final', August 1956 letter is in the possession of Colin Boyne.

The decipherment of Linear B

Ventris's first publication on Linear B, 'Introducing the Minoan language', appeared in the *American Journal of Archaeology*, 44, 1940. The same journal published articles by Alice Kober in 1945, 1946 and 1948, most notably 'The Minoan scripts: fact and theory', 52, 1948, and also Emmett Bennett Jr's article, 'Fractional quantities in Minoan book-keeping', 54, 1950.

The letters written by Ventris to Kober and Bennett were deposited by Bennett in the PASP archives of the University of Texas at Austin, while those written to Sir John Myres are in the Ashmolean Museum archives in Oxford.

The non-technical descriptions of the decipherment by Ventris are: 'Deciphering Europe's earliest scripts', in the *Listener*, 10 July 1952; 'A note on decipherment methods', in *Antiquity*, 27, 1953; and chapter 1 of *Documents in Mycenaean Greek*. The script of his May 1956 BBC broadcast is in the Chadwick Papers at Cambridge University, and his script of another BBC programme, drafted by him in 1956 and broadcast in a modified form after his death, is in the Ventris Papers. His article, 'King Nestor's four-handled cups', describing the famous Pylos 'tripods' tablet, appears in the American journal *Archaeology*, 7, 1954.

The Work Notes appear in facsimile in Ventris's *Work Notes on Minoan Language Research and Other Unedited Papers*, edited by Anna Sacconi (Rome, 1988). This book includes his 1949 questionnaire to scholars and the resulting *Mid-Century Report* ('The languages of the Minoan and Mycenaean civilizations'). Needless to say, this book is tough going even for Linear B specialists.

John Chadwick's *The Decipherment of Linear B*, originally published in 1958, appeared in a second edition in 1967, to which he added a new post-script in 1992 (the current edition); he also wrote *Linear B and Related Scripts* (1987), which contains a chapter on the decipherment. In 1973, Chadwick published a technical article which attempted to explicate the Work Notes, later republished as an appendix in Sacconi's edition of the Work Notes.

The joint publication by Ventris and Chadwick, 'Evidence for Greek dialect in the Mycenaean archives', appears in the *Journal of Hellenic Studies*, 73, 1953.

The Ventris–Chadwick correspondence is in the Chadwick Papers, which also contain Bennett's letters to Ventris and correspondence between Chadwick and other scholars interested in the decipherment.

The proceedings of the 'Minoan Linear B Seminar' at the Institute of Classical Studies have not been published, but a set of minutes for 1954–56 is in the Ventris Papers. The proceedings of the April 1956 colloquium at Gif appear in *Etudes Mycéniennes*, edited by Michel Lejeune (Paris, 1956).

Reviews of the decipherment are too numerous and generally too technical to mention, except for three: A. J. Beattie's notorious pamphlet, *A Plain Guide to the Ventris Decipherment of the Mycenaean Linear B Script* (Berlin, 1958); an objective if somewhat uninspired survey, *The Linear B Decipherment Controversy Re-examined*, by Saul Levin (New York, 1964); and two excellent papers, by Emmett Bennett Jr and Maurice Pope, in *Problems in Decipherment*, edited by Yves Duhoux, Thomas G. Palaima and John Bennet (Louvain-la-Neuve, 1989). Palaima has written several important articles on the decipherment during the last decade or so, and a long article on Alice Kober.

The Minoan and Mycenaean World

As regards Linear B, the chief publication is of course *Documents in Mycenaean Greek*, by Ventris and Chadwick (1956), much added to by Chadwick in a second edition (1973). However, a large proportion is technical. A summary appears in the post-decipherment chapters of *The Decipherment of Linear B*.

Chadwick followed this with a non-technical book, *The Mycenaean World* (1976), which is still in print. More recent books are: *The Aegean Bronze Age* by Oliver Dickinson (1994), *The Discovery of the Greek Bronze*

Age by J. Lesley Fitton (1995), and *Aegean Art and Architecture* by Donald Preziosi and Louise A. Hitchcock (1999).

On Sir Arthur Evans and other archaeologists involved in the Linear B story, see Evans's *The Palace of Minos at Knossos* (1921–35), *From the Silent Earth: The Greek Bronze Age* by Joseph Alsop (1964), *The Villa Ariadne* by Dilys Powell (1973), *Arthur Evans and the Palace of Minos* by Ann Brown (1989), and *Cretan Quests: British Explorers, Excavators and Historians*, edited by Davina Huxley (2000).

Ventris as an architect

Some drawings done by Ventris and his group as students in the 1940s are in the archives of the Architectural Association and the Royal Institute of British Architects. His writings on architecture at this time appear mainly in *Plan*, the magazine of the Architectural Students Association, notably 'Function and arabesque', in *Plan*, 1, and 'Group working', in *Plan*, 2, 1948.

One or two archaeological site drawings by Ventris done at Emborio (Emporio) appear in *Excavations in Chios 1952–55: Greek Emporio*, by John Boardman (1967).

The first part of his report for his 1956 research fellowship appears as 'The handling of architects' information', parts 1 and 2, in the *Architects' Journal*, 15 and 22 November 1956. Dargan Bullivant has a copy of Ventris's February 1956 proposal to the research board for the fellowship.

Ventris's house, 19 North End, is described in 'Keeping the children under', by Mark Girouard, *Country Life*, 12 November 1959. Some plans for the house drawn by Ventris are in the Ventris Papers. The glass-topped desk on which Ventris deciphered Linear B, designed by Marcel Breuer, is in the collections of the Victoria and Albert Museum.

Index

Picture Credits

Frontispiece Camera Press,
photo Tom Blau.
p. 11 Portrait of Arthur
Evans by Sir W. B.
Richmond, 1907,
Ashmolean Museum,
Oxford. Linear B tablet
published by A. Evans in
*American British School
in Athens*, VII, 1900.
p. 17 Dorothea Ventris,
courtesy Renee Ventris.
Ventris family and friends,
Ventris Papers.
p. 22 MV at Stowe. Photo
R. & H. Chapman,
courtesy Tony Meredith.
p. 26 Gold double axe,
Minoan, *c.* 1500 B.C.,
Iraklion Archaeological
Museum. Photo Hirmer.
p. 27 'Room of the Throne'
from A. Evans, *Palace of
Minos at Knossos*, vol. IV,
1935.
p. 28 Highpoint flats,
Highgate, London.
Photo Dell & Wainwright.
© Architectural Review.
p. 34 Greek/Cypriot
inscription. © British
Museum, 2001.

p. 35 Horse tablet
from Chadwick, *The
Decipherment of Linear B*,
1958.
p. 36 Tablet drawing
published in A. Evans,
Palace of Minos at Knossos.
p. 43 MV in the RAF,
Ventris Papers.
p. 46 Christmas card,
Ventris Papers.
p. 54 Cartoon by Oliver
Cox.
p. 55 Architectural sketch,
Architectural Association
archives.
p. 67 Signary order from
Ventris, *Work Notes* (see
Further Reading for
publication details).
p. 77 Sketch of 47
Highpoint by Oliver Cox.
p. 82 Grid from Ventris,
Work Notes.
p. 86 Frequency table from
Ventris, *Work Notes*.
p. 87 Tablet drawing by
MV from *Antiquity*, 1953.
p. 93 Grid from Ventris,
Work Notes.
p. 96 Grid from Ventris,
Work Notes.

p. 105 Syllabary from
archives of PASP (Program
in Aegean Scripts and
Prehistory), University of
Texas at Austin, courtesy
Tom Palaima.
p. 108 Vocabulary list from
Ventris, *Work Notes*.
p. 119 Tripods tablet, Pylos,
13th century B.C. Linear B
signs drawn by MV, first
published in 'King Nestor's
four-handled cups',
Archaeology, 1954.
p. 123 Ventris at work,
Camera Press, photo
Tom Blau.
p. 135 Map of Emporio
published in *Excavations in
Chios* (see Further Reading
for publication details).
p. 136 Ventris family on
holiday, Ventris Papers.
p. 143 MV portrait, Camera
Press, photo Tom Blau.
p. 146 Gif colloquium,
published in proceedings
(see Further Reading for
publication details).
p. 157 Labyrinth drawing
from Lang, *American
Journal of Archaeology*, 1958.